FUNDAMENTALS
OF
PROJECT
MANAGEMENT

James P. Lewis

AMERICAN MANAGEMENT ASSOCIATION

THE WORKSMART SERIES

New York • Atlanta • Boston • Chicago • Kansas City • San Francisco • Washington, D.C.
Brussels • Toronto • Mexico City

Library of Congress Cataloging-in-Publication Data

Lewis, James P., 1941–
        Fundamentals of project management / James P. Lewis.
             p.   cm.—(The WorkSmart series)
        Includes bibliographical references (p.   ).
        ISBN 0-8144-7835-2
        1. Industrial project management.   I. Title.   II. Series.
HD69.P75L488   1995
658.4'04—dc20   94-41740
                                                       CIP

Printing number

10   9

FUNDAMENTALS
OF
PROJECT MANAGEMENT

The WorkSmart Series

CONTENTS

PREFACE: SUCCESSFUL PROJECT MANAGEMENT

Although managing projects has been going on for thousands of years, the practice has only recently been recognized as a discipline in its own right. Suddenly master's-level degree programs are springing up at schools throughout the world, and certificate programs are being offered as well. Not only that, but some organizations have begun to ask their contractors to provide only project managers who have been certified as professionals by the Project Management Institute, the professional society for practitioners.

In today's fast-paced world, organizations that practice sound project management methods have a competitive advantage over those who fly by the seat of the pants. Why? Because competition is rapidly becoming *time-based* as well as *cost-based*. That is, if you can get a product or service to market faster than anyone else, you have an edge on your competition. Further, if you can control the costs of your work better than others, you can sell your products or services at lower margins; "sloppy" management requires that goods be sold at higher margins in order to make sure the business is profitable.

What if you aren't dealing in products or services? The same principle applies. If you are nonprofit or a government agency, you face competition from others who might be able to do your work more efficiently (and at lower cost). In short, we must all learn to work smarter, not harder, in order to survive into the twenty-first century. Managing projects better is one way to achieve that result.

This book gives you a fast-track approach to managing your own projects. You will learn the essential steps in setting up project plans, scheduling your work, and monitoring progress/exercising control to achieve desired project results.

The approach outlined in this book is based on what is considered best practice by experts in the field. If you follow the methods presented here, you will increase the probability that you can meet critical performance, cost, and schedule targets. Admittedly, there is a lot more to project management than can be presented in this short book, but if you learn the essence of the tools, you can go on from there to increase your skill.

CHAPTER 1

AN OVERVIEW OF PROJECT MANAGEMENT

WHAT IS A PROJECT?

What is the difference between project management and managing in general? Aren't they really the same?

The answer, of course, is no. A project is done only once, whereas most jobs are ongoing or repetitive, and managing one-time jobs is different from managing ongoing ones. For one thing, the people who work on a project may be reassigned to other jobs once the project is completed, so the team is temporary. Often the team members do not report to the project manager on a regular basis, meaning that the project manager has no direct authority over them, a situation that presents its own set of problems.

Quality expert Dr. J. M. Juran defines a project as a problem scheduled for solution. This definition forces us to recognize that projects are aimed at solving problems and that failure to define the problem properly is what sometimes gets us into trouble. Interestingly, when you tell project team members that you want to begin planning a project by writing a problem statement, they tend to say, "We don't need to do that. We all know what the problem is."

In my younger days, I was sometimes intimidated by that response. Not any more. My rejoinder is, "If that is true, it will only take five minutes, so let's do it." I have never yet gotten a group to write a problem statement in five minutes, because seldom do people really understand or agree on what the problem is. This failure to achieve a consensus

1

A problem is a gap between where you are and where you want to be, with an obstacle that prevents easy movement to close the gap.

definition of the problem leads to developing the right solution to the wrong problem or to a paralyzing bickering about goals.

To help a team at this point, I offer a definition of a problem. A desired objective is not a problem by itself. The key to a problem is that there is an obstacle that prevents you from closing the gap (achieving your objective) easily. Problem solving consists of finding ways of overcoming or getting around obstacles.

To help flesh out the definition, answer the following questions:

- What is the desired end state or outcome?
- What prevents or makes achieving it difficult?
- How will you know when you have achieved the desired result?

WHAT IS PROJECT MANAGEMENT?

Project management is the planning, scheduling, and controlling of project activities to meet project objectives. The major objectives that must be met include performance, cost, and time goals, while at the same time you control or maintain the scope of the project at the correct level.

project management: **The planning, scheduling, and controlling of project activities to meet project objectives.**

Ideally, the scope of a project should remain constant throughout the life of the job. Naturally, this seldom happens. In most cases the magnitude (scope) of the work increases as a result of overlooked details, unforeseen problems, or an inadequately defined problem. The most common reason for scope changes is that something is forgotten.

Scope generally increases. In fact, about the only time project scope decreases is when the budget is cut and some of the originally planned work is put on hold. The problem with scope changes is that they tend to be small and incremental; if a number of them occur, the project budget or schedule may suffer. This is a fairly common cause of project failures.

performance: The quality of the work being done. **cost:** The cost of project work, directly related to the human and physical resources applied. **time:** The schedule that must be met. **scope:** The magnitude of the work to be performed.

A project manager should advise stakeholders (especially customers) of the impact on the project of a change in scope so that decisions can be made about how to handle such changes. If a customer is told that a requested change will result in a 20% increase in project costs, the customer may opt to defer the change. If the impact is not made clear, the customer may ask for the change, thinking the costs will not increase significantly, and be very dismayed at the end of the job to learn of the true impact. A project manager has a responsibility to keep stakeholders informed about the impact of scope changes on the project, protecting them from surprises at the end of the job and protecting the project manager from being evaluated on original targets rather than on revised ones.

The four project objectives are related to each other by the following equation:

$$Cost = f(P, T, S)$$

What the equation says is that cost is a function (f) of performance (P), time (T), and scope (S). As P and S increase, cost generally increases. The relationship between time and cost, however, is not linear. As a rule, cost increases as the time to do the project decreases below a certain optimum time. That is, there exists a project duration that results in the best performance of all resources. If the duration is shortened, it is often necessary to pay premium labor rates as a consequence. Further, worker errors often increase, resulting in costs for corrections, and productivity often declines. Studies have shown that if a knowledge worker spends twelve hours of overtime on a job, the actual increase in output is equivalent to that normally obtained in two hours of regular work.

In addition, if project work extends beyond an optimum time, costs increase because people are not working efficiently. This relationship is shown in Figure 1-1.

Some senior managers believe that if enough people are thrown at a project, it can be completed in whatever time is desired. This is simply not true, but the idea is the cause of many project fiascos.

Figure 1-1. Cost time curve.

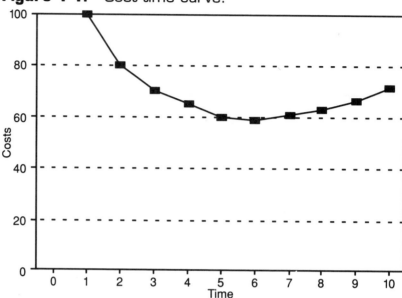

THE HUMAN SIDE OF PROJECT MANAGEMENT

Many factors affect the success of a project. How well was it planned? Was the problem well defined? Was the deadline realistic? Experts agree that there are about ten principal causes of project failure. But what about factors leading to success?

One of the key ingredients is having the right people on the job and managing them appropriately. Note the two elements: having the *right* people and managing them *appropriately*. Both conditions are frequently violated.

The Right People

In many organizations, people are assigned to projects because they are available, not because they are necessarily the right choice for the project. Any personnel manager can tell you that staffing should always be done by first analyzing the requirements of the job, then recruiting the individual who best meets those requirements.

However, projects usually operate in a shared-resource environment. That is, the same employees are used on all projects; when it comes time to start a job, whoever is available is assigned. In fact, pulling a person off one project and assigning her to a new one because she is right for the new job will disrupt the first project—which certainly is not desirable. Nevertheless, assigning the wrong person to a project just because she is available makes even less sense. For one thing, it creates the illusion that the project is properly staffed simply because a "body" is in the position.

Resource allocation is probably the single most important concern of project managers. It is also the aspect that I believe is usually handled worst. Organizations operate today from a lean-and-mean perspective; yet they try to do as much work as they did before they downsized, rightsized, or whatever euphemism is applied to signify that they are now woefully understaffed to do the necessary work.

To address this issue fully would take a book twice the size of this one. Until the problem is recognized and addressed, however, projects will continue to go over budget, miss deadlines, and suffer from poor quality (performance). Furthermore, the scheduling software that is available today to do resource leveling does not address the question of whether the right person is assigned to the job. This is the project manager's responsibility.

The Right Type of Management

The second component of successful project management is managing people appropriately. Unfortunately, individuals often are chosen to become project managers because they are good at their technical discipline but then are given no training in management. It seems to be a prevalent paradigm in the United States that anyone who is good at a technical job can manage. It makes me wonder why we have MBA programs at all.

I personally believe that this failure to train managers is one of the principle causes of business failures in the United

States. The problem is especially common in project management. In fact, there seems to be an inverse correlation between technical performance and management performance. I find that technical people often make terrible managers, although this is by no means always true.

Technical people are (usually) predominantly *thing*-oriented rather than *people*-oriented. They tend to be introverted, meaning that they are oriented toward their internal world of concepts and ideas, rather than toward the external world. So they often deal with people the same way they would deal with things, lamenting that people are not logical, rational, and subject to mathematical analysis.

Some managers still subscribe to an authoritarian view that can be summarized as the KITA principle: If people don't perform, you *Kick* them *In The Anatomy* (you know which part). Their view of people accords with the traditional Theory X outlook described by Douglas McGregor, which sees people as unmotivated (or motivated only by money), untrustworthy, and incapable of thinking and contributing independently; people are seen as members of a herd, requiring a lead cow to guide them.

Such views tend to be self-confirming. The manager behaves as if people were no-goodniks, then finds that they seem to be exactly that. She never realizes that her management style itself has evoked the expected response in her employees. And because she believes that the employees will let her down, she never takes the risk of trusting them, which would have allowed her to find that they actually will perform quite well if given a chance.

Because so much has been written about selecting a management style that is appropriate for a specific follower, I refer the interested reader to those sources and concentrate in this book on the tools of project management, injecting comments, as appropriate, about how people should be dealt with in certain specific situations. One valuable reference is Paul Hersey and Kenneth Blanchard, *The Management of Organizational Behavior: Utilizing Human Resources.*

STEPS IN MANAGING A PROJECT

The actual steps in managing a project are straightforward. Accomplishing them may not be. The model in Figure 1-2 illustrates the steps.

Subsequent chapters of this book elaborate on how each step is accomplished. For now, here is a brief description of the actions involved.

1. *Define the problem.* Identify the problem to be solved by the project. It helps to visualize the desired end result.

Figure 1-2. The steps in managing a project.

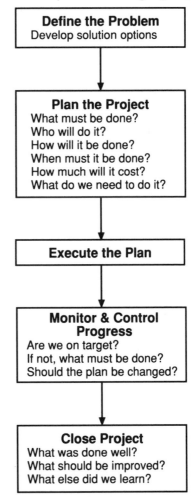

Define the Problem
Develop solution options

Plan the Project
What must be done?
Who will do it?
How will it be done?
When must it be done?
How much will it cost?
What do we need to do it?

Execute the Plan

Monitor & Control Progress
Are we on target?
If not, what must be done?
Should the plan be changed?

Close Project
What was done well?
What should be improved?
What else did we learn?

What will be different? What will you see, hear, taste, touch, or smell? (Use sensory evidence if things can't be quantified.) What client need is being satisfied by the project?

2. *Develop solution options.* How many different ways might you go about solving the problem? Brainstorm solution alternatives (you can do this alone or as a group). Of the available alternatives, which do you think will best solve the problem? Is it more or less costly than other suitable choices? Will it result in a complete or only a partial fix?

3. *Plan the project.* Planning is answering questions— what must be done, by whom, for how much, how, when, and so on. Naturally, answering these questions often requires a crystal ball. We discuss these steps in more detail in Chapters 2 through 4.

4. *Execute the plan.* Once the plan is drafted, it must be implemented. Interestingly, people sometimes go to great effort to put together a plan, then fail to follow it. If a plan is not followed, there is not much point in planning, is there?

5. *Monitor and control progress.* Plans are developed so that you can achieve your end result successfully. Unless progress is monitored, you cannot be sure you will succeed. It would be like using a roadmap to reach a destination but ignoring the highway signs.

Of course, if a deviation from the plan is discovered, you must ask what must be done to get back on track, or— if that seems impossible—how the plan should be modified to reflect new realities.

6. *Close the project.* Once the destination has been reached, the project is finished, but there is a final step that should be taken. Some people call it an audit, others a postmortem. Whatever you call it, the point is to learn something from what you just did. Note the way the questions are phrased: What was done well? What should be improved? What else did we learn? We can always improve on what we have done. However, asking "What did we do wrong?" is likely to make people a bit defensive, so the focus should be on improvement, not on placing blame.

THE PROJECT MANAGEMENT SYSTEM

In order to manage projects successfully, it is necessary to have a system. A full project management system consists of seven components, shown in Figure 1-3. If any one of the seven components is not in place or does not function satisfactorily, then you will have some difficulty managing projects. In fact, most organizations have problems with one or more of the components. Each component is called a *subsystem*, as it is part of the overall system.

Human Factors

The pyramid is underpinned by the human subsystem to show that all other subsystems are dependent on this component for support. A project manager must be able to deal effectively with all of the parts of this subsystem in order to be successful. These include:

- Leadership
- Negotiation
- Team building
- Motivation
- Communication
- Decision making

If there is a deficiency in any of these areas, I suggest that you try to get training in that area. While some people seem to be born leaders, most individuals can improve their leadership skills through training and practice.

Similarly, negotiation is a must-have set of skills for project managers. It is almost universally true that project managers have significant responsibility but little authority. Being able to negotiate with clients for contract terms is sometimes necessary, and you almost always have to negotiate within your organization for scarce resources. In fact, the ability to influence others and the ability to negotiate may well be the

Figure 1-3. The components of a project management system.

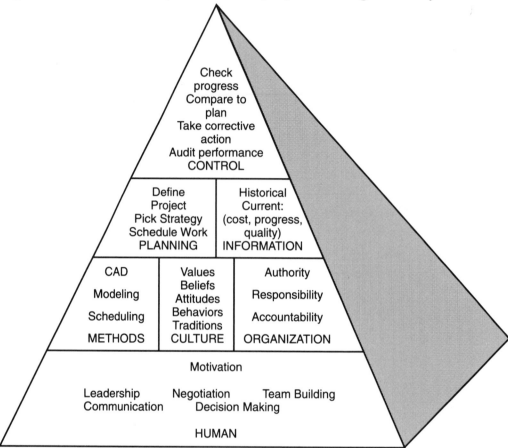

Check
progress
Compare to
plan
Take corrective
action
Audit performance
CONTROL

| Define Project Pick Strategy Schedule Work PLANNING | Historical Current: (cost, progress, quality) INFORMATION |

| CAD Modeling Scheduling METHODS | Values Beliefs Attitudes Behaviors Traditions CULTURE | Authority Responsibility Accountability ORGANIZATION |

Motivation

Leadership   Negotiation   Team Building
Communication   Decision Making

HUMAN

two assets that differentiate between effective project managers and poor or mediocre ones.

Knowing how to turn a group into a team is also essential. Teams don't just happen—they're built! This is especially true when the members of your team have been assigned temporarily to your project but continue to report to their own managers. They have more loyalty to their managers than to your project, and if you are to gain their commitment and support of your project, you have to know how to influence them and turn them into a team. (For a full treatment of building project teams, see my AMACOM book *How to Build and Manage a Winning Project Team.*)

While managers cannot actually provide team members with motivation, they must know how to establish working conditions that draw on whatever motivations a person has. Perhaps more important, they must avoid undermining a person's motivation. Management guru Peter Drucker and others have observed that many organizations do not have as much trouble with unmotivated employees as they do with the fact that they actually destroy motivation by their management practices and/or job environment.

As an example, when I was in India I was told about a project to build a road. Working conditions were terrible. The temperature was typically 90 degrees Fahrenheit, the food at the site was of poor quality, and morale was very low. To add insult to injury, at night the project manager and his immediate staff stayed in a comfortable hotel.

The project finally got into trouble, and the project manager decided to move to the site full-time. Soon the quality of the food improved, along with working conditions. Morale improved as a result, and soon the project was running smoothly. This project manager had no problem with motivation but had one with de-motivation!

Responsibility for ensuring successful communication lies with the *communicator*, not with the person to whom the communication is addressed.

I doubt that there is an organization in the universe that does not have a problem (make that problems) with communication. I know, I know—we managers don't have communication problems. The entire fault lies with followers who simply don't listen!

How many times have you given people assignments, then found them doing the wrong thing? How many times have they told you they were doing what you had instructed them to do, and you argued that they misunderstood? Lost count? Me, too!

Unfortunately, it makes no difference what you intended to communicate. It is how the person interprets what you said that governs her behavior, and if she gets it wrong you will simply have to get her to redo the work. So it is best to get it right the first time. Again, if you have problems communicating with people, get help! Soon!

The meaning of a communication is the response it gets.

One related topic—if you don't know how to make good presentations on your project, you should improve your presentation skills. You may be running the most successful project in the world, but if you can't convey that point to anyone else, it won't matter. You will be judged on what others think is true, rather than on the facts.

Decision making is the remaining skill you need to be an effective project manager. I refer not only to individual decision making but to knowing when a decision is best made by a group and when by an individual. Until recently, autocratic managers made all decisions. Now we hear about participative management and consensus decision making by teams; in some cases, there has been a reversal, with all decisions being made by team consensus.

This is a misunderstanding of participation. There are times when consensus is mandatory and times when it is not, and the project manager must know when each style of decision making is appropriate. Again, for guidelines on when each is appropriate, see my book on project teams, cited earlier.

Methods

Methods refers to the tools of your trade—whatever you use to do the work. For example, CAD (computer-aided-design) might be a tool. Some form of estimating methodology might be a tool. And so on.

Culture

The culture of an organization affects everything you do. It can best be summed up as "the way things are done around here." Culture is formed by the values, beliefs, attitudes, behaviors, and traditions of the people in the company. Note that the corporate culture is affected by *ethnic* cultures as well.

One factor affecting project managers a great deal is that many organizations are becoming more ethnically multicultural. This has always been a problem for international project managers, and it is a growing problem for managers in the United States, where different team members may think differently and have different values because of their varying cultural backgrounds. If we are to manage these differences, we must, first, be aware of them and, second, respect them. The fact that another person's culture causes him to think differently does not make him wrong, but it will cause confusion in the work place until the difference is dealt with.

For example, a manager told me that he had been trying to manage his group more participatively, but an employee from another country had said to him, "Don't give me that participative crap! If you want me to do something, just tell me."

He asked me what to do. I told him to deal with the employee in an autocratic way for now, since that is what he expects and (more important) respects, then to move him gradually toward a participatory style. This is important. You have to deal with people where you find them, then move them to where you want them to be. Trying to deal with them where you want them to be usually fails if the gap is very large.

Organization

Every organization must deal with the assignment and definition of each person's authority, responsibility, and accountability. Too often we see managers trying to delegate responsibility without giving the person any authority. It simply won't work!

Planning

Good project planning is essential for success. Most American companies, however, do not value planning. Managers talk a lot about planning, but the reality is that they would rather do than plan, and it shows. Every organization needs a good methodology for planning projects if it is to be successful.

Information

Most organizations have problems with information on two counts. Good historical data are needed for planning projects, yet most organizations have not kept good records, so they have poor information about their own histories. This is especially true for cost data. There is a rule in many companies that you cannot go above budget on a project. There is another rule that says you cannot come in under budget, either. To achieve such zero variance, projects that are overspending have charges transferred to those that are underspent, thus contaminating both databases and making the data worthless (actually worse than worthless, because they lead to inaccurate budgeting for future jobs). Note also the need for current information. A lot of companies find this to be a problem. They don't have good management information systems (MIS) for projects, only for inventory, payroll, and manufacturing control. In fact, you may have to set up your own system initially, since information systems departments are often slow to develop what you need (if they do it at all). Fortunately, most scheduling software allows you to enter information and track progress yourself. With laptops, you can transmit data from remote sites easily, so this is not the problem that it once was.

Control

In a sense, the only reason you are reading this book is summed up by this one word—control. What are you expected to do as a manager? You are expected to get desired organization results through the management (call that control) of scarce resources. If you aren't in control, you will soon be told about it and steps will be taken to get you in control or to get you out of the way.

The control subsystem is supported by the planning and information subsystems. Both are needed in order to achieve control, because control is exercised by comparing where you are against where you are supposed to be, then taking action to correct any deviations. You need a plan to tell you where you are supposed to be, and you need information to tell you where you are. If either of these is missing, you can't exercise control. More on this in Chapters 7 and 8.

Key Points to Remember

- A project is a problem scheduled for solution.
- If the problem is not defined correctly, you may find the right solution to the wrong problem!
- Focus on desired outcomes. How will you know when you achieve them?
- Try to learn from every project by doing a final audit.

CHAPTER 2

A GENERAL APPROACH TO PROJECT PLANNING

THE IMPORTANCE OF PLANNING

By "shadowing" managers, management professor Henry Mintzberg of McGill University has found that there is a great discrepancy between what they actually do and what management theory says they should do. One area of disparity appears to be in planning. Most managers talk about it, yet many seem reluctant to actually do it.

A major reason for this appears to be cultural. To illustrate, one well-known company arranged to have about 2,000 people spend two weeks planning a major project. When the members of the accounting department multiplied 2,000 people by 80 hours by $50-per-hour labor rates (overhead included) and looked at the total of $8 million, they had cardiac arrest. "You're going to spend $8 million planning the project, and we're not going to get anything for it?" they said. We tend to view planning as a waste, since we don't get anything (meaning anything concrete) for it.

Then, too, in our extremely breakneck, lightspeed world, isn't it really better to just get on with it—to make something happen, anything!—than to spend time sitting around speculating about what might happen and how to deal with it? Isn't it true that we don't really have time to plan?

Fair questions. Let's see if they can be answered logically and definitively.

Planning and Control—Siamese Twins

Managers are supposed to control the application of scarce organization resources to achieve desired results. In a sense, management and control are synonymous.

The question is, what is control? The old connotation implied authoritarianism, domination, the control of people. Another meaning, however, is the definition given in the sidebar—comparing progress to planned performance, then correcting for deviations. That is an *information systems* definition of control. Note that it is your plan that tells you where you are supposed to be; if you have no plan, you have nothing to compare progress against, so without a plan, control is impossible to achieve!

> **Control consists of comparing where you are to where you are supposed to be, then taking corrective action if there is a discrepancy.**

This should be one of the Ten Commandments of management: you must plan in order to control! That is why planning and control have been called Siamese twins—you cannot separate them. Planning is done only so that control can be achieved. No need to do it otherwise. Since control is comparing progress to plan, without the plan there is no control.

I can hear the uproar now! What about fighting fires? You can't plan firefighting, and that is a way of life where we live! You've got to be putting us on.

In the first place, we have fire drills to plan for fighting fires. We have practice sessions or dry runs (planning) to prepare for important business reviews. And it turns out that many fires are the result of not planning properly in the first place. By definition, when you have a fire, something has gone wrong. You are momentarily out of control.

Certainly, there will still be fires to put out, given even the best of planning, but experience shows that they are usually fewer, less serious, and less frequent when good planning is practiced.

> **If you have no plan, you have no control!**

The simple fact is, we have no option but to plan if we want to achieve control of deadlines, of costs, and of ultimate organization performance.

WHAT IS PLANNING?

Planning was defined in Chapter 1 as answering questions. What must be done? Who will do it? How will they do it? How long will it take? How much will it cost? And so on.

Note the tasks involved: estimation (how long and how much cost?); resource allocation (who will do it?); and work identification (what must be done?). Some of these tasks (cost estimating, for example) are so involved that they are done by specialists using special tools—Work Breakdown Structures, CPM/PERT and Gantt schedules, for example.

Strategic vs. Tactical Planning

Most of the focus in project management is on tactical planning. Yet if used with the wrong strategy, tactics are of little help. It is similar to using the right approach to solve the wrong problem.

What is strategy? Simply speaking, strategy is the approach used to do the job. As an example, for thousands of years boats were built with the keel down, that is, in its normal, upright position. That way, when the boat was finished, it could be immediately pushed into the water and floated.

This approach is fine so long as you are building small boats, especially those made of wood. However, during World War II, when Avondale shipyards was called on to build large numbers of military ships, workers found that steel presented new problems. It was hard to weld down in the keel area, partly because you had to stand on your head to do it. In addition, the heavy weight of steel plates made them deform slightly, so when they were finally welded in place, there were some problems with quality.

Those problems could be solved by building the main body of the ship with the keel up—that is, with the ship turned upside down. However, how do you turn a heavy ship over and float it? The answer was to build a large fixture on which

"Any approach to strategy quickly encounters a conflict between corporate objectives and corporate capabilities. Attempting the impossible is not good strategy; it is just a waste of resources."

—BRUCE HENDERSON CEO, Boston Consulting Group

the ship was assembled, then use the fixture to turn the boat over and, eventually, to float it.

This strategy was so effective that it gave Avondale a competitive advantage in the marketplace. No one else could build ships of comparable quality and for such low cost using conventional strategies.

The choice of proper project strategy is important. In construction, for example, prefabricating parts of a structure results in higher quality and faster final construction than is possible when everything is built at the site.

In software, many programming languages allow code to be written in modules; an umbrella code is written to call up the appropriate module when it is needed. This is more efficient than having to rewrite the same code over and over in one program. Further, these modules form building blocks that can be used in other programs, thereby reducing development costs.

Some projects are staffed with a core group of full-time people, and temporary staff are brought in as needed. In others, the entire team is physically colocated so that nobody else in the organization can "steal" them from the critical project.

What Goes Into a Plan?

The minimum ingredients that should be contained in a project plan follow. It is a good idea to keep these in a looseleaf notebook. Initially, the notebook will contain only the plan. As the project is managed, reports, changes, and other documents will be added, so when the project is completed the notebook will contain a complete history of the project, which can be used by others as data for planning and managing their own projects.

One suggestion: Until recently, project notebooks were the only way to document a project completely; I suggest that the notebook be backed up with electronic media. It is very difficult to locate data in a notebook; transferring data to a computer database makes them much easier to access.

The items that make up the project plan include:

- A problem statement.
- A project mission statement (see Chapter 3 for instructions on how to develop a mission statement).
- Project objectives (see Chapter 3).
- Project work requirements (a list of all deliverables, such as reports, hardware, and software). It is a good idea to have a deliverable at each major project milestone so that progress can be measured more easily.
- Exit criteria. These criteria are used to determine when each milestone has actually been reached.
- End-item specifications (engineering specifications, architectural specs, building codes, government regulations, etc.).
- Work Breakdown Structure (WBS). These identify all of the tasks that must be performed in order to achieve project objectives. A WBS is also a good graphic portrayal of project scope (see Chapter 5).
- Schedules (both milestone and working schedules) (see Chapters 5 and 6).
- Required resources (people, equipment, materials, and facilities). These must be specified in conjunction with the schedule (see Chapters 4 and 5).
- Control system (see Chapters 7 and 8).
- Major Contributors. Use a Responsibility Chart for this (see Chapter 4).
- Risk areas, with contingencies if possible (see Chapter 4).

Signoff of the Plan

Once the plan has been prepared, it should be submitted to stakeholders for their signatures. Following are some comments about the meaning of a signature.

stake-holder: Anyone who has a vested interest in the proj-ect. These include contribu-tors, cus-tomers, managers, and finan-cial people.

Suggestions for Handling the Process

• A contributor's signature signifies that the individual is committed to his or her contribution, agrees with the scope of work to be done, accepts the specs as valid, and so on. A signature on the part of a contributor does not mean a guarantee of performance. It is a commitment. Because there are factors outside our control, few of us would like to guarantee our performance. However, most of us would be willing to make a commitment, meaning that we promise to do our best to fulfill our obligations. If a signature is treated as a guarantee, either signers will refuse to sign or they will sign without feeling really committed to the agreement. Neither situation is desirable.

• The plan should be signed in a project plan review meeting, not by mail! Circulating copies for signature by mail seldom works; people may be too busy to read in depth and may miss important points that would have been brought out in a signoff meeting.

• People should be encouraged to "shoot holes in the plan" during the review meeting, rather than wait until problems develop later on. This does not mean that they should nitpick the plan. The objective is simply to ensure that the plan is workable.

Changing the Plan

It would be nice to think that a plan, once developed, will never change. However, that is unrealistic. No one has 20/20 foresight, and unforeseen problems are almost certain to arise. The important thing is to make changes in an orderly way, following a standard change-control procedure.

"Any plan is bad which is not suscep-tible to change."

—BARTOLOMMNO DE SAN CONCORDIO (1475–1517)

If no change control is exercised, the project may wind up over budget, behind schedule, and hopelessly inadequate, with no warning until it is too late.

Suggestions for Handling Changes to the Plan

• Changes should be made only when a significant deviation occurs. A significant change is usually specified in terms of percent tolerances relative to the original targets.

Rule: the people who must do the work should participate in developing the plan.

• Change control is also necessary to protect everyone from the effects of scope creep—changes to the project that create more work. If changes in scope are not identified and managed properly, the project may come in considerably over budget and/or behind schedule.

• Causes of changes should be documented for reference in planning future projects. The causes should be based on fact, not motivated by a desire to blame or punish.

Suggestions for Effective Planning

• Plan to plan. It is always difficult to get people together to develop a plan. The planning session itself should be planned, or it may turn into a totally disorganized meeting like those that plague many organizations. This means that an agenda must be prepared, that the agenda should be time-limited to the degree possible, and that people should be kept on track; if someone gets off on a tangent, the meeting facilitator should get the person back on track as quickly as possible.

The first rule of planning is to be prepared to replan!

• The people who must implement a plan should participate in preparing it. Otherwise, they may feel no sense of commitment to the plan, estimates for their work may be erroneous, and major tasks may be forgotten.

• Because unexpected obstacles will crop up, always conduct a risk analysis to anticipate the most likely ones. Develop Plan B just in case Plan A doesn't work. Why not just use Plan B in the first place? Because Plan A is better but has a few weaknesses. Plan B has weaknesses, also, but they must be different from those in Plan A, or there is no use in considering it as a backup.

Identify project risks, and develop contingencies to deal with them if they occur.

The simple way to do a risk analysis is simply to ask, "What could go wrong?" You should do this for the schedule, work performance, and other parts of the project plan. Sometimes simply identifying risks can help avert them; if that is not possible, at least you can create a backup plan. One caution: if you are dealing with very analytical people, they may go into analysis paralysis here. You are not trying

"Consider the little mouse, how sagacious an animal it is which never en- trusts its life to one hole only."

—PLAUTUS, 254–184 B.C.

to identify every possible risk—just those that are fairly likely.

• Begin by looking at the *purpose* of doing whatever is to be done. Develop a problem statement. All actions in an organization should be taken to achieve a result, that is, to solve a problem. Be careful here to identify what the end user really needs to solve the problem. Sometimes a solution is developed that the project team thinks is right for the client but that is never used, resulting in significant waste to the organization.

• Use the Work Breakdown Structure (discussed in Chapter 4) to divide the work into smaller chunks for which you can develop accurate estimates of duration, cost, and resource requirements.

PROJECT PLANNING STEPS

The basic steps in planning are:

Be sure the project really sat- isfies the customer's needs, rather than being what the team thinks the customer should get!

1. Define the problem to be solved by the project.
2. Develop a mission statement, followed by state- ments of major objectives.
3. Develop a project strategy that will meet all project objectives.
4. Write a scope statement to define project boundaries (what will and will not be done).
5. Develop a Work Breakdown Structure (WBS).
6. Using the WBS, estimate activity durations, re- source requirements, and costs (as appropriate for your environment).
7. Prepare the project master schedule and budget.
8. Decide on the project organization structure— whether matrix or hierarchical (if you are free to choose).
9. Set up the project notebook.
10. Get the plan signed off by all project stakeholders.

QUESTIONS FOR REVIEW

1. If someone tells you there is too little time to plan a project, how would you defend your conviction that planning is necessary?

    a. Tell the person that a project plan will save time in the long run.
    b. Prove that without a plan, there can be no control.
    c. Both a and b.
    d. Only b.

2. What is the difference between strategy and tactics?

    a. Strategy is an overall approach to a project. Tactics are specific steps taken to implement strategy.
    b. Strategy is the political approach taken to manage a project. Tactics are the moves you make to beat a competitor.
    c. Both a and b.

3. Why is it necessary to get people to participate in planning a project? Why can't the project manager just do it for them?

    a. If the project manager plans the project and anything goes wrong, everyone will blame him or her for all the problems.
    b. Without participation, people are not committed to a plan.
    c. Participation in planning helps ensure that things aren't forgotten and that estimates are accurate.
    d. All of the above.
    e. Only c.

4. Of what value is a project notebook?

    a. It allows you to protect yourself from people who change their minds about what they want once the project is started.
    b. It keeps all data in one place.
    c. It provides a complete track record of the project and can be used for planning future projects.
    d. All of the above.
    e. Only b.

5. Why is it a good idea to use an electronic database to back up a project notebook?

    a. It is difficult to access data in hard-copy form.
    b. An electronic database is more technologically advanced.
    c. Using an electronic database allows you to keep data confidential.

6. If someone asks for a change in the scope of your project, what should you do?

    a. Tell the person to get lost.
    b. Explain the impact of the change and ask if the person still wants you to proceed.
    c. Ask why the person didn't think of it before you got started.

The answers are listed in the Appendix.

Key Points to Remember

- If you have no plan, you have no control.
- The people who must execute the plan should participate in preparing it.
- Have the plan signed off in a meeting, not through the mail. A signature from a contributor is a commitment, not a guarantee.
- Keep all project documentation in a project notebook, but back it up with an electronic database if possible.
- Use exit criteria to determine when a milestone has actually been achieved and the project is ready to proceed to the next step.
- Require signatures for changes in scope in order to alert everyone as to the impact of the change on project costs, deadlines, etc.
- Risk analysis is part of planning. For every risk identified, develop a contingency plan, when possible.

CHAPTER 3

DEVELOPING THE PROJECT MISSION, GOALS, AND OBJECTIVES

IMPORTANCE OF THE MISSION STATEMENT

Developing a problem statement and a mission statement go hand in hand. It could easily be argued that a project's mission is to solve an identified problem. In fact, I some-times find the development of the two statements to be a bit circular; as I work on defining the problem I begin to see the mission more clearly, and vice versa. It would be nice if the mind worked in nice linear fashion, but this is not always the case, so it does not pay to argue about the order in which these statements should be developed.

Often, achieving a mission requires solving one major prob-lem plus a host of smaller ones. In the 1960s, President John F. Kennedy gave NASA its mission: to put a man on the moon and return him safely to earth by the end of the decade. The budget was essentially unlimited. Within the program Kennedy outlined were a host of projects, each with its own mission.

"If you don't know where you're going, how will you know when you get there?" This questions sums up the reason some projects go astray. The mission statement is developed to prevent confusion on the part of the project team concern-ing the direction the project should take. After it is created, the mission statement should be used to set goals and objectives, to make decisions, and to select team members—

A mission statement provides the basis for which goals and objectives can be set and for making decisions, taking actions, hiring employees, etc.

that is, to answer any and every question that arises in the course of executing the project.

Note the word *used*. Once the mission statement is developed, it should be used. This seems obvious; yet many organizations seem to forget the mission statement after it is written. Perhaps it is because project managers tend to then go into the firefighting mode and forget the mission. Like the old joke, they have forgotten that the objective is to drain the swamp because they are too busy fighting the alligators.

In their book *In Search of Excellence*, Peters and Waterman say that one characteristic of excellent companies is that they "stick to their knitting." Two points are of significance here. First, the company knows that it knits rather than crochets. Second, it sticks to knitting and does not wander off into the world of crochet.

This approach seems to be a far cry from that used in the 1960s by many organizations, which formed conglomerates for diversity under the belief that if you are really a good manager, you can manage anything. That assumption has been challenged in recent years, for the data simply don't support it. Nevertheless, it persists.

A company mission statement provides a focus that can help you select the right projects to do, and the project mission statement should keep you focused on the desired project outcomes.

SATISFYING THE CUSTOMER IN PROJECT MANAGEMENT

A primary concern of an organization is to satisfy its customers.

The quality movement that began in the 1980s made managers aware that a primary concern of an organization, whether a business or a not-for-profit agency, is to satisfy its customers. The same can be said for project teams. A project is conducted to solve a problem; it will be judged based on how well it meets the needs of end users, regardless of whether it came in on time and on budget. Slevin and Pinto have written that when a project comes in on time and

Quality Function Deployment (QFD) is a method of examining product or service features and comparing them to customer needs and wants to see how they correlate.

budget but fails to meet the needs of the customer, its managers have committed an Error of the Third Kind (see Dennis Slevin, *The Whole Manager,* AMACOM Books, p. 313). This type of error seems to happen far more frequently than one would expect.

To avoid this problem, many organizations today are using Quality Function Deployment (QFD) to help translate customer needs and wants into product or service features, together with Concurrent Project Management, which gets customers, vendors, contributors, and other parties to the project together from concept through completion.

QFD is a method of examining product or service features and comparing them to customer needs and wants to see how they correlate. The idea is to be certain that you give the customer those features that satisfy his needs without giving him more than necessary, which would simply add cost to the product without adding value for the customer. For a fuller treatment of the subject, see Yoji Akao, *Quality Function Deployment: Integrating Customer Requirements Into Product Design,* Productivity Press.

Concurrent Project Management (often called Concurrent Engineering) is a response to the throw-it-over-the-wall approach that has been practiced for many years. In the traditional approach, marketing talked to customers, defined the product or service, and threw the specifications over the wall to the developers, who then developed the product, threw it over the wall to manufacturing (or whoever had to produce it), and went on to something else.

Often the producers would find problems and would throw the design back over the wall to the developers to fix; this might happen several times. Finally, the customer got the goody, found it lacking, and sent it back. Such failure to deliver products and services that meet the needs of customers costs us our customers.

If project managers do not insist on interfacing directly with customers, this type of failure is likely. In developing a mission statement for a project, therefore, it is imperative to

Concurrent Project Management gets all workers affected by a project involved from concept through completion so that they are informed and can participate in issues that affect them.

talk with customers to find out what their needs are and how they view quality (that is, what they mean by quality), and then set out to meet those requirements. Involvement of the key members of the project team (preferably, the entire team) is also essential. Technical teams must not decide what they think is best for the customer without really trying to understand her needs. As an example, E. F. Schumacher pointed out in his book *Small Is Beautiful* that Westerners tend to install the latest technology in developing countries, whether or not it best meets the needs of the country's industry and whether or not the infrastructure necessary to support it exists.

THE MISSION IDENTIFICATION PROCESS

A mission statement should answer three questions:

1. What do we do?
2. For whom do we do it?
3. How do we go about it?

The first question requires that we focus on objectives, deliverables, or end-results. The second asks us to identify our customers. The third makes us think about how we are going to achieve the desired results—what kind of processes or methods we will employ. Naturally, the answer to this question will be very broad.

As an example, suppose a project team is set up to develop a funding program for a local public television station. The team members see their mission as follows:

> Our mission is to develop a program to solicit donations from area viewers to support the operation of WXYZ during the coming year. This is to be achieved through advertising, public relations campaigns, the aid of local clubs and service organizations, and special fund-raising programs aired by WXYZ.

It is not necessary to answer the second question explicitly in this case, since it is obvious who the client is. This is not always true, so it is generally a good idea to be explicit in identifying the customer.

It is also a good idea to get the entire team to participate in developing the statement. By doing so, you get better buy-in, understanding, and commitment to the mission than is possible when the team leader develops the statement unilaterally.

Developing a mission statement that can be accepted by an entire team takes time—anywhere from an hour to months, with a day being fairly typical. Managers often think that they cannot afford to spend so much time on a mission statement; much better just to draft a statement and communicate it to everyone, they think.

I have found that this is not true. Either you pay now or you pay later. I believe you are better off paying now. If everyone does not understand the mission of the team, you are in for major problems later on.

Some managers also fall into the trap of thinking that it is almost impossible to gain consensus with groups. It is true that it takes a lot of time. However, consensus means that everyone is able to support the majority position, even if each person does not entirely agree with it. Where full support is needed, it is a good idea to take the time in the beginning to get everyone aligned with the direction in which the team is going. Failure to do so means that individual contributors will go off on tangents (or even at right angles to the desired direction), and their work will have to be done over. Most projects cannot afford such waste.

EXAMPLE OF PROBLEM AND MISSION STATEMENTS

Suppose you were managing the project to write this book. You might write a statement of the problem being addressed as follows:

There is no currently existing book on project management that is an easy read. Most available books are too technical and impractical. The obstacle to developing this book is the difficulty of translating some concepts into practical language.

Next, you can write a mission statement as follows:

The mission of this project is to produce a book on project management that translates technical concepts into down-to-earth language for the practitioner or other individual who wants a quick overview of project management.

Developing Project Objectives

Once a mission statement has been developed, project objectives can be written. Objectives are much more specific than the mission statement itself. They define results that must be achieved in order for the overall mission to be accomplished.

An objective specifies a desired end result to be achieved. A task is an activity performed to achieve that result. An objective usually is a noun, whereas a task is a verb.

I may want to finish this chapter by 10 o'clock this morning. That is my desired outcome or result—my objective. The way I achieve that objective will be to perform a number of tasks. These might include typing text into my computer, reviewing some other literature on the topic about which I am writing, calling a colleague to ask a question for clarification, and printing out the chapter, proofing it, and entering some revisions into my computer.

The following acronym may help you remember the essential qualities that characterize a statement of objectives. We say that an objective must be *smart*, each letter standing for a particular aspect:

Specific
Measurable
Attainable
Realistic
Time-limited

W. Edwards Deming has raised some serious questions about the advisability of trying to quantify goals and objectives. He argued in *Out of the Crisis* that there is no point in setting quotas for a manufacturing process. If the system is stable, he suggested, then there is no need to specify a goal; you will get whatever the system can produce. A goal beyond the capability of the system can't be achieved.

On the other hand, if the system is not stable (in the statistical sense of the word), there is still no need to specify a quota, because there is no way to know what the capability of the system is.

In project work, we can ascertain the capability of a person by looking at his past performance, but unless we have a large number of samples for each person, we have no way of knowing exactly what he can do, since output varies every time a task is performed. Further, it does no good to base a quota on what someone else has done; the quota must be valid for the person who is going to do the task this time.

We all know that some people are capable of more output than others. So the measurement and attainability aspects of goal- or objective-setting are very difficult to determine. I have found the following two questions to be useful both in setting objectives and in monitoring progress toward those objectives:

1. *What is our desired outcome?* This is called the outcome frame. It helps keep you focused on the result you are trying to achieve, rather than on the effort being expended to get there.
2. *How will you know when you achieve it?* I call this the evidence question; it is very useful for establishing exit criteria for objectives that cannot be quantified.

Some Examples of Objectives

- Our objective is to develop a one-minute commercial to solicit contributions to WXYZ to air on local TV stations by June 5, 199X.

It is helpful to assess risks of failure of the following:
• **The schedule**
• **The budget**
• **Project quality**
• **Customer satisfaction**

• Our objective is to raise $600,000 from local viewers by September 18, 199X.

The Nature of Objectives

In the examples of objectives that I have given, I do not say how they will be achieved. I consider an objective to be a statement that tells me what result is to be achieved. The *how* is problem solving, and I prefer to keep that open so that solutions can be brainstormed later. If the approach is written into the objective statement, it may lock a team into a method that is not really the best.

ASSESSING PROJECT RISKS

Once objectives have been established for areas such as scheduling, budgeting, project quality, and customer satisfaction, plans can be developed for how to achieve them. Unfortunately, the best plans sometimes don't work. One safeguard in managing projects is to think about the risks of failure that could sink the job. This can be done for critical objectives and for other parts of the plan. The simplest way to conduct a risk analysis is to ask, "What could go wrong?" or "What could keep us from achieving our objective?"

It is usually best to list risks first, then to think about contingencies for dealing with them. One approach is to divide a flipchart page in half and have the group brainstorm the risks, which are tabulated down the left side of the page. You then come back and list contingencies—things you can do about risks if they do materialize.

One benefit of doing a risk analysis in this manner is that it can help you to minimize risks. When you cannot eliminate a risk, you can at least have a backup plan. It is common to find that unexpected risks can throw a project into a tailspin.

One reminder: you are not trying to identify every possible risk, just some of the more likely ones. This point should be made for team members who are highly analytical or who have a tendency to be negative in general. Also, risk analysis is always done with a positive thrust—that is, you are asking, "If it happens, what will we do about it?" You don't want people to play "Ain't it awful!"

PLANNING EXERCISE

Choose a project that you are going to do or have just started. Answer the questions that follow to the best of your ability. If you need to confer with others to answer some of them, fine. Remember, the people who have to follow the plan should participate in preparing it.

1. What are you trying to achieve with the project? What need does it satisfy for your customer? Who exactly is going to actually use the project deliverable(s) when it is finished? (That is, who is your real customer?) What will distinguish your deliverable from those already available to the customer?
2. Write a problem statement, based on your answers to question 1. What is the gap between where you are now and where you want to be? What obstacles prevent easy movement to close the gap?
3. Now write a mission statement, answering the three basic questions: What are we going to do? For whom are we doing it? How will we go about it?
4. Talk to your customer about these issues. Do not present your written statements to her. Rather, see if you can get confirmation of your mission statement by asking open-ended questions. If you don't, you may have to revise what you have written.

Key Points to Remember

- A mission statement helps the team stay focused on what it is supposed to do.
- The mission statement should be developed by the entire team when possible.
- Once the mission has been defined, goals and objectives can be set.
- Risk analysis should always be done with a positive thrust, asking, What will be done to deal with any risk that materializes?

CHAPTER 4

USING THE WORK BREAKDOWN STRUCTURE TO PLAN A PROJECT

I have said that planning is answering some questions, among which are "What must be done?" "How long will it take?" and "How much will it cost?" Planning the *what* is vital. One frequent reason projects fail is that a significant part of the work is forgotten. For example, one construction project manager experienced a serious cost overrun because he forgot to include the cost of clearing land in his project budget. In addition, once tasks have been identified, the time and resources necessary to accomplish them must be determined. This process is called *estimating*.

> Expressing his frustration over the cost of the B-2 bomber, a congressman said, "I want it to cost what they tell me it's going to cost." The job spanned ten years. Do you suspect that the scope changed a few times during that period? That technology grew exponentially (especially in computers)? This gentleman probably thinks that it is possible to have an exact estimate!

Errors in estimating how long tasks will take and what it will cost to do them are a leading cause of project failures. Missing cost targets is a common cause of stress and recrimination in project management.

The most useful tool for accomplishing these tasks is the Work Breakdown Structure (WBS). The idea behind the WBS is simple: A complicated task is subdivided into several

THE CASE OF THE $600,000 ERROR

When Charlie took over a project to build a wing of a hospital, he picked up a job already in progress. The former project manager had left to take another job. Charlie soon learned why.

As he examined the plan left by his predecessor, Charlie got worried. Something was wrong, but he couldn't put his finger on it. Just one of those gut feelings you sometimes get when things don't look quite right.

Charlie told his new boss about his concern and was surprised to find that Tom agreed. "I've had the same concern," Tom said. "Hang in there until you find it."

It was several days before Charlie realized what was wrong. Workers were clearing the wing site of trees and rocks, but the cost of the work was nowhere in the plan! He did a quick estimate of the site preparation cost, and his heart sank. The figure was almost $600,000, and the original estimate to do the entire job was only $2 million!

Together, Charlie and Tom called a meeting with the board of the hospital. When told the news, the board members physically paled, then sent the two out of the room. "I'm probably going to get fired for this," Tom told Charlie outside, as he paced around in the hall. "You just came here, so I think you're safe."

After an agonizing half hour, the board called them back in. "Well, we're committed to do this job," the chairman said, "so we'll have to find the money somewhere."

He paused.

"Before you leave, gentlemen, do you have any more surprises for us?" he asked.

This is one of the ten most common causes of project failures—forgetting to plan for some aspect of the work.

smaller tasks. This process can be continued until the task can no longer be subdivided, at which time you will probably find it easier to estimate how long each small task will take and how much it will cost to perform.

For example, if I want to clean a room (see Figure 4-1), I might begin by picking up clothes, toys, and other things that have been dropped on the floor. I could use a vacuum cleaner to get dirt out of the carpet. I could wash the windows and wipe down the walls. I might also dust the furniture. All of these tasks are subtasks performed to clean the room.

As for vacuuming the room, I might have to get the vacuum cleaner out of the closet, connect the hose, plug in the machine, push it around the room, empty the bag, and put it back in the closet. These are even smaller tasks to be performed in accomplishing the subtask called vacuuming. The diagram in Figure 4-1 shows how this might be portrayed in WBS format.

Note that we do not worry about the sequence in which work is performed when we do a WBS. That will be worked out when we do a schedule. However, you will probably

Figure 4-1. Work breakdown structure for room-cleaning project.

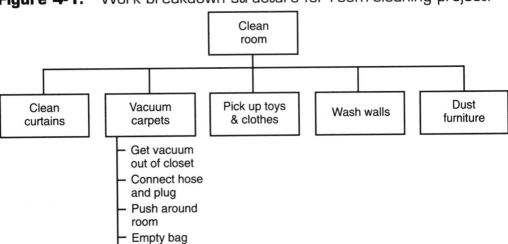

find yourself thinking sequentially, in spite of this suggestion, since it seems to be human nature to do so. The main
idea of doing a WBS is to capture all of the tasks. If you find
yourself and other members of your team thinking sequentially, don't be too concerned, but don't get hung up on
trying to diagram the sequence, or you will slow down the
process of task identification.

The typical WBS has three to six levels, and these can be
named as shown in Figure 4-2. It is, of course, possible to
have projects that require a lot more levels. Twenty levels is
considered to be the upper limit; such an undertaking would
constitute a huge project. Note that level 1 is called the

Figure 4-2.   Names for work breakdown structure
levels.

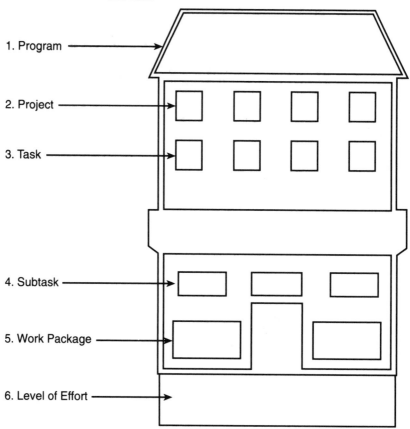

1. Program
2. Project
3. Task
4. Subtask
5. Work Package
6. Level of Effort

program level. The difference between a program and a project is just one of degree.

When you are developing products, the task level (as I have called it) will be a component of the overall thing being developed. For example, if we are designing an airplane, we might develop the fuselage, wing, navigation system, engines, and so on. While these are actually things, it is still an *activity* to develop them; I therefore call all of the boxes verbs, even though they result in things (nouns). It really does not pay to get hung up on semantics except when very precise terminology is needed for clear communication. Then you must adhere to a system as defined by the user.

GUIDELINES FOR DEVELOPING THE WBS

One important question to ask when constructing a WBS is when to stop breaking down the work. The general guideline is that you stop when you reach a point at which you can estimate to the desired degree of accuracy or at which the work will take an amount of time equal to the smallest units you want to schedule. If, for instance, you want to schedule to the nearest day, break down the work to the point at which each task takes about a day to perform. If you are going to schedule to the nearest hour, then you stop when task durations are in that range.

Remember the rule that the people who must do the work should participate in planning it? That applies here. Usually a core group identifies top-level parts of the WBS; then those parts are refined further by other members of the team and integrated to obtain the entire WBS.

The WBS should be developed before the schedule. In fact, the WBS is the device that ties the entire project together. It allows you to assign resources and to estimate costs and resources, and it shows the scope of the job in graphic form. Later, as you track the project, you can identify the work as being such-and-such a box in the WBS.

There is at least one software package, SuperProject Expert™, that will print a WBS after schedule data have been entered. That is a nice feature, since it gives a graphically attractive WBS, but you should make a rough drawing before using the scheduling software. The reason is quite simple: until everyone has agreed that all tasks have been identified, it is misleading to develop a schedule. You cannot be sure the critical path identified by a partial schedule will be the same for the full schedule.

There are a number of approaches to developing the WBS. Ideally, you proceed top-down, after developing a good problem statement and mission statement. The mind does not always operate in such nice linear fashion, however, and as you develop the WBS, you may find that it helps you understand the job better. For that reason, I am not a purist about following specific procedures. Do what works best for you.

The WBS does not have to be symmetrical. That is, all paths need not be broken down to whatever level you stop at. Since the rule is to break work down to a level sufficient to achieve the estimating accuracy you desire, one path may take six levels, while another may need only three.

USES OF THE WBS

As I have said, the WBS is a good way to show the scope of a job. If you have ever given someone an estimate for project cost or time and seen the person have a cardiac arrest, you know that it is generally because the person sees the project as being much simpler than it is. When you show a project in WBS form, it is clear to most individuals why the job costs so much. In fact, sometimes the planning group itself is overwhelmed by the complexity and magnitude of the WBS. If it impresses these pros, think of the impact on the outsider.

Assigning responsibility for tasks is another important use of the WBS. Each task to be performed should be assigned to a specific person. These assignments can then be listed on a separate form, often called a Responsibility Chart (see Figure 4-3).

ESTIMATING TIME, COSTS, AND RESOURCES

Once the work is broken down, you can estimate how long it will take. But how do you do this? Suppose I ask you how long it will take to sort a well-shuffled deck of playing cards into numerical order by suit. How would you answer that question?

The most obvious way is to actually sort the deck several times and get a feeling for how long it takes. If you don't have a deck of cards handy, you might think about it, imagine how long it would take, and give me an answer. People generally suggest anywhere from two to ten minutes. My tests indicate that about three minutes is the average for most adults.

Figure 4-3.   A project responsibility chart.

Project xyz	Work Breakdown Structure Tasks							
Contributors	501	502	503	504	505	506	507	508
John W.	1	2	2					
Susan K.	2			1				
Tom R.					1	1		
Mary L.				2			1	
Alice Q.	2	2						
Andy D.								1
Kathy G.								2
Paul T.					2	2	2	

Key: 1 = Actual responsibility for task; 2 = Contributor

Parkinson's Law: Work expands to take the time allowed.

Suppose, however, that we were to give the cards to a child about four or five years old. It might take a lot longer, as the child is not that familiar with the sequence in which cards are ordered and perhaps is not even that comfortable with counting yet. We therefore reach a very important conclusion: you cannot do an estimate without considering who will actually perform the task. Second, you must base the estimate on historical data or on a mental model. Historical data are best.

We usually use average times to plan projects. That is, if it takes three minutes on average for adults to sort a deck of cards, I would use three minutes as my estimate of how long it would take during execution of my project. Naturally, some tasks will take longer than the time allowed and some will probably take less. Overall, they should average out.

We must be careful not to penalize workers who perform better than expected by loading them down with excessive work.

That is the idea, anyway. Parkinson's Law discredits this notion, however. Parkinson said that work always expands to take the time allowed. That means that tasks may take longer than the estimated time, but they almost never take less. One reason for this phenomenon is that when people find themselves with some time left, they tend to refine what they have done. Another is that if they turn work in early, they may be expected to do the same work faster the next time, or they may be given additional work to do. This possibility discourages people from handing work in ahead of time; if they are penalized for performing better than the target, they will quit doing so.

We also have to take into account *variation*. If the same person sorts a deck of cards over and over, we know the sort times will vary. Sometimes the sorting will take two minutes; other times it will take four. The average may be three, but we expect that half the time it will take three minutes or less and half the time it will take three minutes or more. Very seldom will it take exactly three minutes.

An exact estimate is an oxymoron!

The same is true for all project tasks. The reason? Forces outside the person's control. The cards are shuffled differently every time. The person's attention is diverted by a loud noise outside. He drops a card while sorting. He gets tired. And so on.

Can you get rid of the variation? No way.

Can you reduce it? Yes. Through practice, by changing the process by which the work is done, and so on. But it is important to note that the variation will always be there, and we must recognize and accept it.

Improving Estimating Ability

The more times you do something, the better you get at estimating how long it and similar tasks will take the next time you do them. This suggests that very inexperienced people will typically make bad estimates—which is usually the case.

Edward Russo and Paul Schoemaker, in their book *Decision Traps,* relate a story about Royal Dutch Shell that provides a nice solution to the problem. Royal Dutch Shell found that its senior geologists were considerably better at analyzing geological surveys to predict where to drill for oil than were its recently graduated geologists. Even the senior geologists have a fairly low "hit rate," but for new graduates the outcomes were much worse.

A project should be audited at major milestones, with spreads no greater than three months. Beyond that time, memories are not reliable.

Royal Dutch Shell started a program in which new graduates were given survey data of areas that had already been drilled. They were then asked to predict the results of drilling in these areas. They were then told what had actually happened. In a very short time, the new graduates were predicting as accurately as the old-timers.

This illustrates a very important point: learning does not take place unless there is feedback on results. If an organization never looks at results and studies the causes for those outcomes, the people involved tend to repeat the same mistakes.

The Hazards of Estimating

Consider the case of Karen. One day her boss stopped by her desk at about 1 o'clock. "Need for you to do an estimate for me," he told her. "Promised the Big Guy I'd have it for him by 4 o'clock. You with me?"

Karen nodded and gave him a thin smile. The boss described the job for her. "Just need a ballpark number," he assured her. Given so little time, Karen could only compare the project her boss described to one she had done about a year before. She added a little for this and took a little off for that, put in some contingency to cover her lack of information, and gave the estimate to the boss. After that, she forgot all about the job. Two months passed. Then the bomb was dropped. Her boss appeared, all smiles. "Remember that estimate you did for me on the xyz job?"

She had to think hard to remember, but as her boss droned on, it came back to her. He piled a big stack of specifications on her desk. "It's your job now," he told her and drifted off again into manager dreamland.

As she studied the pile of paper, Karen felt herself growing more concerned. There were significant differences between this set of specs and what her boss had told her when she did the estimate. "Oh well, I'm sure he knows that," she told herself. She managed to work up a new estimate for the job on the basis of the real specs. It was almost 50% higher than the ballpark. She checked her figures carefully, assured herself that they were correct, and went to see her boss.

One of the ten primary causes of project failures is that ballpark estimates become targets.

He took one look at the numbers and went ballistic. "What are you trying to do to me?" he yelled. "I already told the old man we would do it for the original figure. I can't tell him it's this much more. He'll kill me."

"But you told me it was just a ballpark number you needed," Karen argued. "That's what I gave you. But this is nothing like the job I quoted. It's a lot bigger."

"I can't help that," her boss argued. "I already gave him the figures. You'll have to find a way to do it for the original bid."

Naturally, you know the rest of the story. The job cost even more than Karen's new estimate. There was a lot of moaning

Guidelines for documenting estimates:
- **Show the percent tolerance that is likely to apply.**
- **Tell how the estimate was made and what assumptions were used.**
- **Specify any factors that might affect the validity of the estimate (e.g., will it still be valid after six months?).**

and groaning, but in the end, Karen survived. Oh, they did send her off to a course on project management. Hoping, no doubt, that she would learn how to estimate better in the future.

Can you fault Karen for anything? Well, perhaps. If she failed to tell her boss that a ballpark estimate may have a tolerance of perhaps 25% to as much as 100%, then she allowed him to think the estimate was better than it was. Also, she should have documented all working assumptions, explaining how she did the estimate, to what project it was compared, and so on. Then, if management still pulled a whammy on her, at least she would have had some protection. In fact, it is impossible to make sense of any estimate unless these steps are taken, so this should be standard practice.

EXERCISE

Following is a list of tasks involved in a project to prepare for a camping trip. Draw a WBS that places the tasks in their proper relationship to each other. The solution is shown in the Appendix.

- Arrange for supplies and equipment.
- Select camp site.
- Make site preparations.
- Make site reservation.
- Arrange time off from work.
- Select route to site.
- Prepare menu for meals.
- Identify source of supplies and equipment.
- Load car.
- Pack suitcases.
- Purchase supplies.
- Arrange Camping Trip (project).

Key Points to Remember

- A WBS is used to subdivide a large project into smaller tasks, making it easier to estimate durations, resource requirements, and costs.
- A major cause of project failure is that something is forgotten. The WBS, together with a review of the plan, is one aid to help prevent this problem.
- A WBS does not show the sequence in which work is done. A schedule is used for that purpose.
- When possible, estimates should be based on experience. An estimate should also take into account who is going to do the task.
- Another major cause of project failure is that ballpark estimates are sometimes misused and become targets.
- An estimate should always be qualified: What is its accuracy? How was the estimate prepared? What limitations does it contain?

CHAPTER 5

SCHEDULING PROJECT WORK

Project management is not just scheduling.

One of the primary features that distinguishes project management from general management is the special attention to scheduling. Remember from Chapter 1 that Dr. J. M. Juran describes a project as a problem scheduled for solution.

Unfortunately, some people think that project management is nothing but scheduling. This viewpoint is incorrect. Scheduling is just one of the tools used to manage jobs and should not be considered the primary one.

One common tendency is for people to acquire scheduling software, of which there is an abundance, and think that it will make them instant project managers. They soon find that that idea is wrong. In fact, it is nearly impossible to use the software effectively unless you understand project management (and scheduling methodology in particular).

I do have one suggestion about software. Whatever you pick, get some professional training in how to use it. In the early days of personal computers there was a pretty significant difference between the low-end and the high-end software that was available. The low-end packages were pretty easy to use, whereas the high-end ones were not.

The gap between low- and high-end software has closed to the point that there is no longer a significant disparity in ease of use between them. They are all difficult to use, and the training materials (tutorials and manuals) that come with the software are often not very good. In addition, it is hard to find time to work through a tutorial without being interrupted repeatedly, which means that self-learning is difficult. The most efficient way to learn is to take a class.

Before signing up for a class, check out the instructor's knowledge of project management. There are people teaching the software who know very little about project management itself; when you have questions, they won't be able to answer them. You should expect to spend from two to three days of classroom time becoming really proficient with the software—a good investment, considering the time the software can save you in the long run.

A BRIEF HISTORY OF SCHEDULING

Until around 1958, the only tool for scheduling projects was the bar chart (see Figure 5-1). Because Henry Gantt developed a complete notational system for showing progress with bar charts, they are often called Gantt charts. They are simple to construct and to read, and they remain the best tool for communicating to team members what they need to do in given time frames. Although arrow diagrams tend to be too complicated for some teams, it is often helpful to show such a diagram to the people doing the work so that they understand interdependencies among tasks and why it is important that they complete certain tasks on time.

Figure 5-1. A sample bar chart.

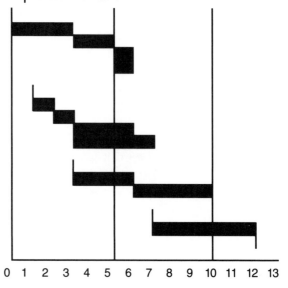

CPM: Critical Path Method PERT: Performance Evaluation & Review Technique

Gantt charts have one serious drawback—determining the impact of a slip of one task on the rest of the project is very difficult. That is, if Collect Data in Figure 5-1 gets behind, it is hard to tell how it will affect the rest of the work, because the bar chart does not show the interdependencies of the work.

To overcome this problem, two methods of scheduling were developed in the late 1950s and early 1960s that used arrow diagrams to capture the sequential and parallel relationships among project activities. One method was called Critical Path Method (CPM), developed by du Pont; the other, Performance Evaluation and Review Technique (PERT), was developed by the Navy and the Booze, Allen and Hamilton consulting group. Although it has become customary to call all arrow diagrams PERT networks, strictly speaking, the PERT method makes use of probability techniques, whereas CPM does not. In other words, using PERT allows you to calculate the probability that an activity will be completed by a certain time, whereas CPM does not.

NETWORK DIAGRAMS

Arrow diagrams like those in Figure 5-2 are used to show the sequence in which work is performed. In these diagrams Task A is done before B, while Task C is done in parallel with them.

The network in the bottom half of Figure 5-2 uses activity-on-arrow notation, in which the arrow represents the work being done and the circle represents an event. An event is binary; that is, it has either occurred or it has not. An activity, on the other hand, can be partially complete. Note that this is a special use of the word *event*. We speak of a football game as an event, even though it spans time. In scheduling terminology, however, an event is a specific point in time where something has just started or has just been finished.

The network in the top half of Figure 5-2 uses activity-on-node notation, in which the work is shown as a box or node

Figure 5-2. Arrow charts.

An activity-on-node network.

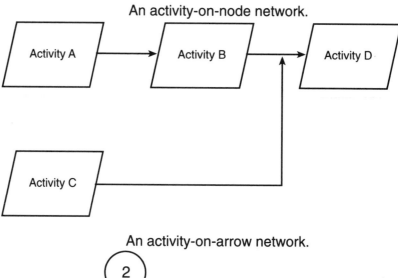

An activity-on-arrow network.

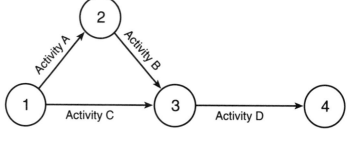

and the arrows show the sequence in which the work is performed. Events are not shown in activity-on-node networks unless they are milestones—points in the project at which major portions of the work are completed.

Why two forms of diagrams? Probably a tyranny to confuse the initiate. Actually, it simply happens that the schemes were developed by different practitioners.

Is one better than the other? No. They both get the same results in figuring out when work is supposed to be completed. Both forms are still used, although activity–on–node is used a bit more than the other, because much of today's personal computer software is programmed to use node notation.

The main advantage of using CPM or PERT is that they allow you to predict if it is possible to meet an important

The critical path is the longest path through a project network and determines the earliest date on which work can be completed. All activities on the critical path must be completed as scheduled, or the end date will begin to slip—one day for each day a critical activity is delayed.

project completion date and when various tasks must be finished in order to meet that deadline. Further, you can tell which tasks have some leeway and which do not. In fact, both CPM and PERT determine the location of the *critical path* (the longest series of activities that can't be done in parallel) and thus governs how early the project can be completed.

THE REASON FOR SCHEDULING

Naturally, the primary reason for scheduling a project is to ensure that an imposed deadline can be met. Because the critical path method helps identify the activities that will determine the end date, it also offers guidance on how the project should be managed.

It is easy to get carried away with scheduling and to spend all of your time updating, revising, and so on. The scheduling software in use today should be viewed as a tool, and managers should not become slaves to the tool.

It is also very easy to create schedules that look good on paper but won't work in practice. The main reason this occurs is a lack of resources with which to do the work when it comes due. In fact, unless resource allocation is handled properly, schedules are next to useless. Fortunately, today's scheduling software handles resource allocation fairly well. I leave discussion of the methods used to the software manuals and in this book simply examine how networks are used to show us where we need to manage.

I am often told that scope and priorities change so often in a given organization that it doesn't make sense to spend time finding critical paths. There are two points worth considering here. One is that if scope is changing often in a project, not enough time is being spent doing up-front definition and planning. Scope changes most often occur because something is forgotten during the planning stage. Better attention to what is being done in the beginning usually reduces scope creep.

Second, if priorities are changing often, management does not have its act together, and the organization may be trying to tackle too much work for the number of resources available. We all have "wish lists" of things we personally want to do, but we have to put some of them on hold until time and/or money become available. The same is true of organizations. Experience shows that when individuals are working on many projects, productivity suffers. For example, one company found that when it stopped having people work on multiple projects, their productivity doubled! That obviously is highly significant.

DEFINITIONS OF NETWORK TERMS

activity: An activity always consumes time and may also consume resources. Examples include paperwork, labor, negotiations, machinery operations, and lead times for purchased parts or equipment.

critical: An activity or event that must be achieved by a certain time, having no latitude (slack or float) whatsoever.

critical path: The critical path is the longest path through a network and determines the earliest completion of project work.

event: Beginning and ending points of activities are known as events. An event is a specific point in time. Events are commonly denoted graphically by a circle and may carry identity nomenclature (words, numbers, alpha-numeric codes, etc.).

milestone: An event that represents a point in a project of special significance, usually the completion of a major phase of the work. A project review is often conducted at that time.

network: Networks are called arrow diagrams. They provide a graphical representation of a project plan showing the relationships of the activities.

What does CPM have to do with this? Knowing where the critical path is in a project allows you to determine the impact on the project of a scope or priority change. You know which activities will be affected most severely and what might need to be done to regain lost time. It also allows informed decision making by management. Thus, CPM, used properly, can be an invaluable tool.

Constructing an Arrow Diagram

As I pointed out in Chapter 4, before scheduling is done, a Work Breakdown Structure (WBS) consisting of from two to twenty levels should be developed. To illustrate how a schedule is constructed from a WBS, we consider a simple job of maintaining the yard around a home. The WBS is shown in Figure 5-3.

It is appropriate for this WBS to schedule the tasks at the lowest level. This, however, is not always true. It is possible, for example, that you may break down the work to level 6 but enter only those activities up to level 5 into the schedule.

Figure 5-3.   Work breakdown structure for yard project.

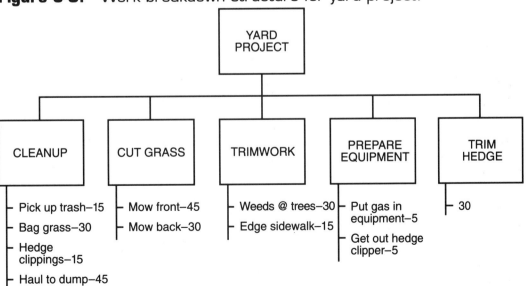

Don't schedule in more detail than you can manage.

The reason for this is that you may not be able to keep level six tasks on schedule; you may not be able to manage that tightly. So you schedule at a level that you can manage. This follows the general rule that you should never plan (or schedule) in more detail than you can manage. Some projects, such as overhauling a large power generator, are scheduled in increments of hours. Others are scheduled in days, while some big construction jobs are scheduled to the nearest month.

While planning in too much detail is undesirable, if you plan in too little detail, you might as well not bother. As a practical example, a manager told me that his people wanted to create schedules showing tasks having twenty-six-week durations. He protested that they would never complete such schedules on time. They would back-end load them, he argued.

What he meant was that there is a lot of security in a twenty-six-week task. When the start date comes, if the person doing the task is busy, she might say, "I can always make up a day on a twenty-six-week activity. I'll get started tomorrow." This procrastination may continue until she realizes she has delayed too long. Then there is a big flurry of activity as she tries to finish on time. All the work has been pushed out to the end of the twenty-six-week time frame.

A good rule of thumb to follow is that no task should have a duration much greater than four to six weeks.

A good rule of thumb to follow is that no task should have a duration much greater than four to six weeks. A twenty-six-week task can probably be broken down into five or six subtasks. This approach generally keeps people from back-end loading.

There are two ways to develop a schedule. One is to begin at the end and work back until you arrive at the beginning. The second method is to start at the beginning and work toward the end. Usually, it is easiest to start at the beginning.

The first step is to decide what can be done first. Sometimes several tasks can start at the same time. In that case, you simply draw them side-by-side and start working from there. Note the progression in the diagram in Figure 5-4. I

Figure 5-4. CPM diagram for yard project.

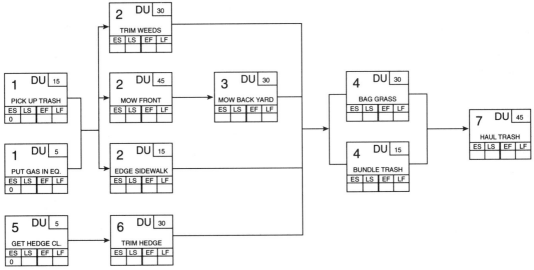

have numbered the boxes according to the steps taken to place them. In other words, all boxes with a 1 beside them were placed in the diagram in step 1, and so on. Note that it sometimes takes several iterations before the sequencing can be worked out completely.

This small project might be thought of as having three phases: preparation, execution, and cleanup. There are three preparation tasks: pick up trash, put gas in equipment, and get out hedge clipper. The cleanup tasks include bagging grass, bundling clippings, and hauling trash to the dump.

Schedules should be developed according to what is logically possible; resource allocation should be done later. This yields the optimum schedule.

In doing this schedule diagram, I have followed a basic rule of scheduling—to diagram what is logically possible, then deal with resource limitations. For a yard project, if no one is helping me, then there really can be no parallel paths. On the other hand, if I can enlist help from the family or neighborhood youth, then parallel paths are possible. The rule I suggest is that you go ahead and schedule as if it were possible to get help. This is especially important to remember in a work setting, or you will never get a schedule put together. You will be worrying about who will be available to do the work and end up in analysis paralysis.

Another rule is to keep all times in the same increments— minutes or days, for example.

Another rule is to keep all times in the same increments. Don't mix hours and minutes—schedule everything in minutes, then convert to hours and minutes as a last step. For this schedule, I have simply kept everything in minutes.

I suggest that you draw your network on paper and check it for logical consistency before entering anything into a computer scheduling program. If the network has logical errors, the computer will just give you a garbage-in, garbage-out result, but it will look impressive, having come off a computer.

It is also important to remember that there is usually no single solution to a network problem. That is, someone else might draw the arrow diagram a bit differently than you have done. Parts of the diagram may have to be done in a certain order, but often there is flexibility. For example, you can't deliver papers until you have printed them, so if the diagram shows this, it is wrong. There is no single right solution, but a diagram can be said to be wrong if it violates logic.

The network for the yard project could get a lot more complicated. You could add *edge front sidewalk* and *edge back sidewalk*. You could talk about trimming around trees in both front and back. And so on. But there is no need to make it too complicated. We don't usually try to capture exactly how we will do the work, just the gist of it.

It is hard to tell if a network is absolutely correct, but it can be said to be wrong if logic is violated.

The next step is to figure out how long it will take to do the job. Time estimates for each task are made by using history—remembering how long each activity has taken in the past. Remember, though, that the estimate is valid only for the individual who is going to do the task. If my daughter, who is sixteen, does the lawn mowing using a push mower, it will probably take less time than if my son, who is only twelve, tackles the job. (In Chapter 6, we discuss how to find the critical path through the network, which helps you figure out how long the project will take.)

Figure 5-5. Work breakdown structure for room-cleaning project.

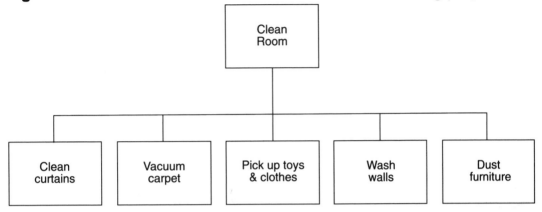

EXERCISE

For the WBS in Figure 5-5, draw an arrow diagram. One solution is shown in the Appendix.

Key Points to Remember

- Project management is not just scheduling.
- Arrow diagrams allow an easier assessment of the impact of a slip on a project than do Gantt charts.
- Schedule at a level of detail that can be managed.
- No task should be scheduled with a duration much greater than four to six weeks. Subdivide longer tasks to achieve this objective.

CHAPTER 6

SCHEDULING COMPUTATIONS

The critical path is the longest path through a project network. It therefore determines the earliest completion for the work.

Once a suitable network has been drawn, with durations assigned to all activities, it is necessary to determine where the longest path is in the network and whether it will meet the target completion date. Since the longest path through the project determines minimum project duration, if any activity on that path takes longer than planned, the end date will slip accordingly. Because of its importance, this path is called the *critical path*.

Normally, you would let a computer do these computations for you, so you may wonder why it is necessary to know how to do them manually. My belief is that unless you know how the computations are done, you do not fully understand the meanings of float, early and late dates, and so on. Further, you can easily fall prey to the garbage-in, garbage-out malady. So here is a brief treatment of how the calculations are done by the computer. (For most schedules, the computer has the added bonus of converting times to calendar dates, which is no easy task to do manually.) First, consider what we want to know about the project. If it starts at some *time = zero,* we want to know how soon it can be finished. Naturally, in most actual work projects, we have been told when we must be finished; that is, the end date is dictated. Further, the start date for the job is often constrained for some reason: resources won't be available, specs won't be written, or another project won't be finished until that time. So scheduling usually means trying to fit the work between two fixed points in time. Whatever the case, we want to know how long the project will take to complete; if it won't fit into the required time frame, then we will have to do something to shorten the critical path.

Failure to consider resource allocation in scheduling almost always leads to a schedule that cannot be achieved.

In the simplest form, computations are made for the network on the assumption that activity durations are exactly as specified. However, activity durations are a function of the level of resources applied to the work, and if that level is not actually available when it comes time to do the work, then the scheduled dates for the task cannot be met. It is for this reason that network computations must ultimately be made with resource limitations in mind. Another way to say this is that resource allocation is necessary to determine what kind of schedule is actually achievable. Failure to consider resources almost always leads to a schedule that cannot be met.

The first step in network computations is to determine where the critical path is in the schedule and what kind of latitude is available for noncritical work under ideal conditions. The ideal situation is one in which unlimited resources are available, so the first computations made for the network are done ignoring resource requirements. This is the method that will be described in this chapter; for information on resource allocation methods, the reader is referred to scheduling software manuals.

NETWORK RULES

Initial schedule computations are made on the assumption that unlimited resources are available. This yields the best-case solution.

Two rules are applied to all networks in order to compute network start and finish times. (Other rules are sometimes applied by the scheduling software itself. These are strictly a function of the software and are not applied to all networks.)

Rule 1: Before a task can begin, all tasks preceding it must be completed.

Rule 2: Arrows denote logical precedence. The length of the arrow or its angular direction have no significance. (It is not a vector but a scalar.)

BASIC SCHEDULING COMPUTATIONS

Scheduling computations in this section are based on the network in Figure 6-1. First, let us examine the node boxes

Figure 6-1. CPM diagram for yard project.

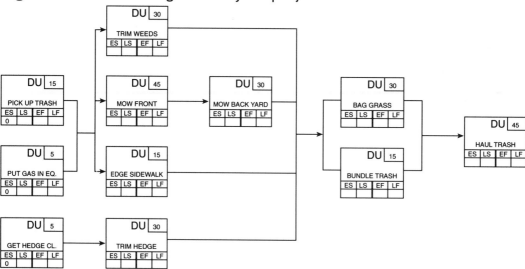

in the schedule in Figure 6-2. Each contains the notations *ES, LS, EF, LF,* and *DU.*

$$ES = \text{Early Start}$$
$$LS = \text{Late Start}$$
$$EF = \text{Early Finish}$$
$$LF = \text{Late Finish}$$
$$DU = \text{Duration (of the task)}$$

Forward Pass Computations

Consider a single activity in the network, such as picking up trash from the yard. It has a duration of fifteen minutes. Assuming that it starts at time = zero, it can finish as early as fifteen minutes later. We therefore can enter *fifteen* in the cell labeled EF.

Putting gas in the mower and the weed whacker takes only five minutes. The logic of the diagram says that both of these tasks must be completed before we can begin trimming weeds, cutting the front grass, and edging the sidewalk. The cleanup task takes fifteen minutes, whereas the gas activity takes only five minutes. How soon can the following activi-

Figure 6-2.   Forward pass computations for yard schedule.

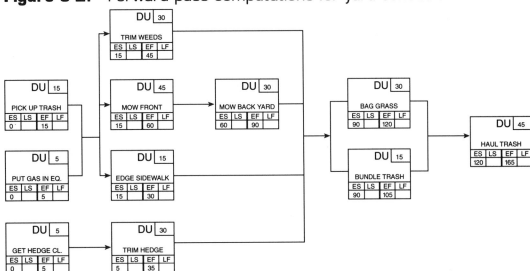

ties start? Not until the cleanup has been finished, since it is the longest of the preceding activities.

In fact, then, the Early Finish for cleanup becomes the Early Start for the next three tasks. It will always be true that the latest Early Finish for the earlier tasks becomes the Early Start for subsequent tasks. That is, the longest path determines how early subsequent tasks can start.

Following this rule, we can fill in Earliest Start times for each task, as shown in Figure 6-2. This diagram shows that the project will take a total of 165 minutes to complete, if all work is conducted exactly as shown. We have just performed what are called *forward pass computations* to determine Earliest Finish times for all activities. Computer programs do exactly the same thing and also convert the times to calendar dates, making quick work of the computations.

The Earliest Start for a task is the latest Late Finish of preceding tasks. That is, the longest path determines the earliest that a subsequent task can be started.

Rule: When two or more activities precede another activity, the earliest time that the final activity can be started is the larger of the durations of the activities preceding it.

The time determined for the end or final event is the earliest finish for the project in working time. Once weekends, holidays, and other breaks in the schedule are accounted for, the end date may be considerably later than the earliest finish in working time.

Backward Pass Computations

A backward pass is made through the network to compute the latest start and latest finish times for each activity in the network. (See Figure 6-3.) To do this, we must decide how late the project can finish. By convention, we generally don't want a project to end any later than the earliest possible completion; to stretch it out longer would be inefficient.

We also won't insist (for now) that our yard project end earlier than the earliest possible finish calculated in the preceding section. If we want to finish earlier we will have to redraw the network or shorten some activities (by applying more resources or working more efficiently, for example). For now, we will accept the 165-minute working time and let it be the Latest Finish for the project.

Figure 6-3.   CPM diagram for yard project (filled in).

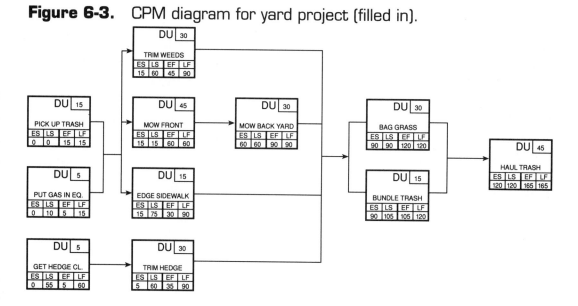

When doing backward pass calculations, always use the smallest number for the LF of previous activities.

If Hauling Trash has a Late Finish of 165 minutes and has a duration of 45 minutes, what is the latest that it could start? Subtracting 45 from 165 leaves 120 minutes, which is the Latest Start for the task. Proceeding in this manner, we get LS times for Bagging Grass and Bundling Clippings of 90 and 105 minutes, respectively. One of these two numbers must be the LF time for each of the preceding activities. Which one?

Well, assume we try 105 minutes. If we do that, Bagging Grass could start as late as 105 minutes, since as soon as earlier tasks are finished, subsequent tasks can begin. But if we add 30 minutes for Bagging to the 105-minute ES time, we will finish at 135 minutes, which is later than the 120 minutes previously determined, and we will miss the 165-minute end time for the project.

When you are doing backward-pass calculations, the Latest Finish for a preceding task will always be the smallest of the Late Start times for the subsequent tasks. (A simpler way to say this is: Always use the smallest number!)

> *Rule:* When two or more activities follow a third activity, the latest time that the earlier activity can be achieved is the smaller of the times.

When an activity has no float, it is called *critical*, since failure to complete work as scheduled will cause the end date to slip.

All of the activities that have ES/LS or EF/LF times that differ are said to have *float*. For example, Trim Weeds has an ES time of fifteen minutes and a LS time of sixty minutes, giving it forty-five minutes of float.

Now examine the path that includes activities highlighted by bold lines. Each activity has the same ES/LS and EF/LF times. There is no *float* on this path. By convention, an activity with no float is called *critical,* and a total path with no float is called a *critical path*; if any of the work on this path falls behind schedule, the end date for the project will slip accordingly.

Some of the tasks in Figure 6-3 have the same EF and LF times, as well as the same ES and LS times. These tasks are on the critical path. In the figure, they are shown with bold outlines to indicate exactly where the critical path lies.

Critical path activities have no latitude. They must be completed as scheduled or the entire project will take longer than the allotted 165 minutes. Knowing where the critical path is tells a manager on which areas to focus; the other tasks have latitude, or float. This does not mean that they can be ignored, but they have less chance of delaying the project if they encounter problems. The Edge Sidewalk task, for example, has an ES time of fifteen minutes and a LS time of seventy-five. The difference between the two is sixty minutes, which is the float for the task. What good is the float? Well, we know we can start the task as late as seventy-five minutes into the job and still finish the project on time. If your son is doing this task, he can watch a sixty-minute television program during that time and still get his Edging task done on time.

Remember, too, that the times are all estimates. This means that tasks may take more or less time than we have scheduled. So long as they do not take longer than the scheduled time plus the available float time, the job can be done on time. Critical tasks, which have no float, must be managed in such a way that they take the scheduled time. This is usually done by adjusting the resources (effort) applied, either by assigning more resources or working overtime (increasing resources in either case).

It is bad practice to schedule a project so that overtime is required to meet the schedule, since if problems are encountered, it may not be possible to work more overtime to solve them.

Adjusting the resources is not always possible. Applying overtime often increases errors, leading to rework, which may mean that you don't get the job done any faster than if you had simply worked a normal schedule. Further, there is always a point of diminishing returns when you add bodies to a task. At some point the workers just get in one another's way, actually slowing work down rather than speeding it. Overtime should be kept in reserve in case it is needed to resolve problems, and it is never a good idea to schedule a project so that overtime needs to be worked just to meet the original schedule.

Another point of great importance: all members of the project team should be encouraged to keep float times in reserve as insurance against bad estimates or unforeseen

Once you have used up the float on a task, it becomes part of the critical path.

problems. People tend to wait until the latest possible start time to begin tasks; then, when problems occur, there is no float left and they wind up missing the end date. When a task takes longer than originally planned, it can impact the end date for the entire project, since once a task runs out of float, it becomes part of the critical path. In fact, the true meaning of the word critical is that it has no float. It must be done on time.

USING THE NETWORK TO MANAGE THE PROJECT

The point of developing a CPM diagram is to use it to manage the project. If this is not done, scheduling is simply a worthless exercise. So here are some pointers that I have found helpful in managing my own jobs:

• Try to stay on schedule. It is always harder to catch up than to stay on target to begin with.

• Keep float in reserve in case of unexpected problems or bad estimates.

• Apply whatever effort is needed to keep critical tasks on schedule. If a task on the critical path can be finished ahead of schedule, do it! Then start the next task.

• Avoid the temptation to perfect everything—that's what the next generation product or service is all about. I don't mean that it is okay to do your work sloppily or that you shouldn't do your best. I mean that you should not be tempted to make your work perfect. Realistically, you will never reach perfection.

• Estimates of task durations are made on the basis of the output of particular people. If someone else is actually used, you may have to adjust durations accordingly. This is especially true if the person is less skilled than the intended resource.

• No task should be scheduled with a duration much greater than four to six weeks. As I noted in Chapter 5, if you do allot greater time spans for tasks, people will develop a false sense of security and are likely to put off starting, under the assumption that they can always make up the time. If a task has a duration greater than six weeks, it is a good idea to subdivide it, creating an artificial break if necessary. Then review progress at that point. That will help keep it on target.

• If the people doing the work did not develop the network, explain it to them and teach them the meaning of float. Give them a bar chart to work to; it is much easier to read a bar chart than a network diagram. Show them that if they use up float on a task, then subsequent tasks may become critical, leaving the people who must do those activities under great pressure.

• It is possible to shorten a task by adding resources, reducing the scope of the task, doing sloppy (poor quality) work, being more efficient, or changing the process by which the task is done. With the exception of doing sloppy work, all of these methods may be acceptable. A reduction in scope must be negotiated with your customer, of course.

• Scheduling is done initially on the assumption that you will have the resources you planned on having. If people are shared with other projects or if you plan to use the same person on several tasks, you may find that you have overloaded her. Modern software generally will warn you that you have overloaded your resources and may be able to help you solve the problem.

CONVERTING ARROW DIAGRAMS TO BAR CHARTS

While an arrow diagram is essential to do a proper analysis of the relationships among the activities in a project, the best working tool is the bar chart. Those people doing the work will find it much easier to know when they are supposed to start and finish their jobs if you give them a bar chart. The arrow diagram in Figure 6-3 has been converted to a bar chart in Figure 6-4, making use of what was learned about the schedule from the network analysis.

Figure 6-4. Bar chart schedule for yard project.

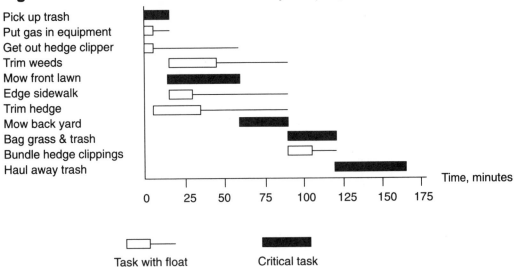

The critical path in the bar chart is shown with solid black bars. Bars with float are drawn hollow, with a line trailing to indicate how much float is available. The task can end as late as the point at which the trailing line ends.

This is fairly conventional notation. Scheduling software always allows a bar chart to be printed, even though a CPM network is used to find the critical path and to calculate floats. One caution: Many programs display the critical path in red on a color monitor and may color tasks that have been started with green or blue. When these are printed on a black-and-white printer, all of them may look black, implying that they are all critical and confusing the people trying to read them.

It is usually possible to have the computer display shading or cross-hatching instead of color so that when the schedule is printed in black and white, there will be no ambiguity.

Because most scheduling programs don't create good bar charts when times are in minutes, the bar chart in our example was created manually using Corel Draw. Printouts from scheduling packages usually look pretty similar.

CONSTRAINING THE END DATE

I have said previously that most projects have the end date imposed, by contract, market necessity, customer need, or whatever. In addition, the start date for the project may be determined by further constraints—people or equipment won't be available until a certain time, perhaps.

Typically, when you pin down the start date for a project and calculate the end date for the network, the initial solution won't meet the required end date. That means that the project duration must be reduced. If you plug the required finish into the last activity's LF cell, rather than letting the computer make the EF and LF the same (which is conventional analysis), the LF will actually be earlier than the EF for that activity. That means it automatically has *negative float,* since the float is always LF minus EF. We say that the activity is *supercritical* under that constraint.

In this case, you will find that all activities on the original critical path now have the same negative float as the final activity and that those activities that originally had float now have it reduced by an amount equal to the negative float on the critical path. If those tasks had a total float less than the amount of the negative float on the supercritical path, then those activities also will become supercritical.

Such an analysis allows you to determine exactly how much each task duration must be shortened. This can be done according to the procedures I discussed in a previous section of this chapter (adding resources, for example). Not all software allows you to do this analysis, but when it does, it helps you to see where the network must be adjusted.

EXERCISE

For the network in Figure 6-5, calculate the early and late times and the float available on noncritical activities. Which activities form the critical path? Answers are in the Appendix.

Figure 6-5. Network for exercise.

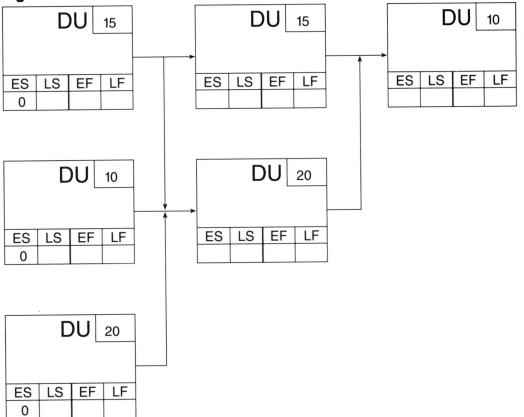

Key Points to Remember

- The critical path method is a way of locating the longest path through a project and determining how much latitude (commonly called float) is available on noncritical tasks.
- Failure to consider resource allocation in scheduling usually yields a schedule that cannot be met.
- A forward pass calculation is used to determine early times for activities, and a backward pass is used to find late times.
- When an activity has no float, it is called a *critical* activity. Once the float available to a task is used up, that activity becomes critical.
- Float can be used to compensate for estimating variability, unforeseen problems, and other causes of delay.
- It is bad practice to schedule a project so that overtime is needed to meet original target dates, as this leaves no latitude for handling any problems that might occur later.

CHAPTER 7

PROJECT CONTROL AND EVALUATION

Every step described up to now has had one purpose—to achieve control of the project. This is what is expected of a project manager—that organization resources be managed in such a way that critical results are achieved.

The word *control* has two meanings; it is important that we use the one that is appropriate in today's world. Control can imply domination, power, command. We control people and things through the use of that power. When we say "jump," people ask, "How high?" At least they used to. It doesn't work that way today.

I have discussed the fact that project managers often have a lot of responsibility but little authority. Let's examine that fact and see if it is really a problem.

I have asked several corporate officers (presidents and vice presidents) this question: "Since you have a lot of authority, does that authority guarantee that people will do what you want done?"

Uniformly, they answer, "No."

"What does get them to do what you want done?"

"Well, in the end analysis, they have to want to do it," they say.

"Then what does your authority do for you?" I ask.

"Well, it gives me the right to exercise sanctions over them, but that's all."

Having authority does not guarantee that you will be able to get people to do your bidding. In the end, people have to be

There are two kinds of authority: power over people and the ability to make decisions and to act unilaterally.

willing to do as you ask, which means that you have to understand what motivates people so that you can influence them to do what needs to be done.

There is a second kind of authority that has to do with taking actions unilaterally—that is, without having to get permission first. In this sense of the word, many companies do have a lot of organizational problems. I meet project managers who have project budgets in the millions of dollars (as much as $35 million in one case), yet who must have all expenditures approved. Now if a project plan and budget have been approved before the work was started and if the project manager is spending within the approved limits of the plan, why should more signatures be needed? Only if a deviation from the plan is going to result should approvals be required, and then the plan should be revised to reflect those changes.

Consider the messages being sent to these managers. On one hand, they are being told, "We trust you to administer $35 million of our money." On the other hand, they are told, "But when you spend it, you must have every expenditure approved by someone of higher authority." One is a positive message: We trust you. The other is negative. Which do you think comes through loud and clear? You bet! The negative.

Interestingly, we complain that people in organizations won't take more responsibility for themselves, then we treat them as if they are irresponsible and wonder why they don't behave responsibly!

The first meaning of control, then, connotes power. Another meaning, which was introduced in an earlier chapter, suggests that control is comparing progress to plan so that corrective action can be taken when a deviation from planned performance occurs. This definition implies the use of information, rather than power, as the primary ingredient of control. Thus, we talk about management information systems, and indeed, these are the essence of what is needed to achieve control in projects.

Unfortunately, many organizations have management information systems that are good for tracking inventory, sales, and manufacturing labor but are not good for tracking projects. Where such systems are not in place, you will have to track progress manually.

ACHIEVING TEAM MEMBER SELF-CONTROL

Ultimately, the only way that a project can be under control is to have every member of the project team in control of his or her own work. A project manager can achieve control at the macro level only if control is achieved at the micro level. However, this does not mean that you should practice micro-management! It does mean that you should set up conditions under which every team member can achieve control of his or her own efforts. To do this requires five basic conditions.

1. *Clarify for every team member what her objective is.* Note the difference between tasks and objectives, which was discussed in Chapter 3. State the objective, and explain to the employee (if necessary) what the purpose of the objective is. This allows the individual to pursue the objective in her own way.

2. *Have each worker prepare a personal plan for doing the required work.* Remember, if you have no plan, you have no control. This applies at the individual level, as well as the overall project level.

3. *Ensure that all workers have the skills and resources needed for the job.* The need for resources is obvious; in addition, some workers may require training if they lack the necessary skills. Certainly, when no employee with the required skills is available, it may be necessary to have team members trained.

4. *Provide direct feedback to each worker.* If feedback is given in some roundabout way, workers cannot exercise self-control. On the other hand, if a team member is building a wall, she can measure the height of the wall,

compare that to the planned performance, and know whether she is on track or not.

5. *Define clearly for each individual her authority to take corrective action when there is a deviation from plan—and it must be greater than zero authority!* If the worker has to ask the project manager what to do every time a deviation occurs, the project manager is still controlling. (In addition, if very many people have to do this, it puts a real burden on the project manager.)

CHARACTERISTICS OF A PROJECT CONTROL SYSTEM

All good project control systems have several characteristics in common. These include:

• *A focus on what is important.* The control system must focus on project objectives. The aim is to ensure that the project mission is achieved. To do that, the control system should be designed with these questions in mind:

- What is important to the organization?
- What are we attempting to do?
- Which aspects of the work are most important to track and control?
- What are the critical points in the process at which controls should be placed?

Control should be exercised over what is important. On the other hand, what is controlled tends to become important. Thus, if budgets and schedules are emphasized to the exclusion of quality, only they will be controlled; the project may well come in on time and within budget at the expense of quality. Project managers must monitor performance carefully to ensure that quality does not suffer.

• *A system for taking corrective action.* A control system should focus on response. If control data do not result in action, then the system is ineffective. That is, a control system must use deviation data to initiate corrective action; otherwise, it is simply a monitoring system, not a control system. If you are driving and realize that you have somehow gotten on the wrong road, but you do nothing to get back on the right road, you are not exercising control.

One caution here, though. I once knew a manager whose response to a deviation was to go into the panic mode and begin micro-managing. He then got in the way of the people who were trying to solve the problem and actually slowed them down. Had he left them alone, they would have solved their problem much faster.

• *An emphasis on timely responses.* The response to control data must be timely. If action occurs too late, it will be ineffective. This is frequently a serious problem. Data on project status are sometimes delayed by four to six weeks, making it useless for taking corrective action. Ideally, information on project status should be available on a real-time basis. In most cases, however, that is not possible. For many projects, weekly status reports are adequate.

When people fill out time reports each week without having written down what they did daily, they are writing fiction. Such made-up data are almost worse than none at all.

Ultimately, you want to find out how many hours people actually work on your project and compare that figure to what was planned. This means that you want accurate data. Some people may fill out weekly time reports without having kept track of their daily working times. This results in a bunch of fiction, since most of us cannot remember with any accuracy what we did a week ago.

As difficult as it may be, you need to get people to record their working times daily so that the data will mean something when you collect them. What's in it for the workers? Perhaps nothing. However, their better estimates (made as a result of collecting accurate information on this project) will help everyone who works on the next project. In any case, you need accurate data, or it isn't worth the effort at all.

When information collection is delayed for too long, the manager may wind up making things worse instead of better. Lags in feedback systems are a favorite topic for systems theorists. The government's attempts to control recessions and inflation sometimes involve long delays, as a result of which the government does the exact opposite of what it should have done, thus making the economic situation worse.

One important point about control: If every member of the project team is practicing proper control methods, then weekly reports are just checks and balances. This is the desired condition.

DESIGNING THE RIGHT SYSTEM

One system is not likely to be correct for all projects. You may need a scaled-down system for small projects and a beefed-up one for large ones. Generally, a control system adequate for a large project will overwhelm a small one with paperwork, while a system that is good for small projects won't have enough "clout" for a big project.

The *Kiss* Principle

No problem is so big or so complicated that it can't be run away from.

—CHARLIE BROWN (Charles Schultz, *Peanuts*)

Follow the *Kiss* principle—keep it simple! The smallest control effort that achieves the desired result should be used, and any control data that are not essential should be eliminated. One common mistake is to try to control complex projects with systems that are too simple.

To keep control simple, it is a good idea to check periodically that reports that are generated are actually being used for something by the people who receive them. We sometimes create reports because we believe the information in them should be useful to others, but sometimes we are just kidding ourselves. To test this, send a memo with each report asking people to let you know if they want to continue receiving similar reports. You may be surprised to find that no one uses some of your reports. Those should be dropped completely or revised to meet user needs.

PROJECT EVALUATION

As the dictionary says, to evaluate a project is to attempt to determine if the overall status of the work is acceptable in terms of intended value to the client once the job is finished. Project evaluation appraises the progress and performance of a job and compares it to what was originally planned. That evaluation provides the basis for management decisions on how to proceed with the project. The evaluation must be credible in the eyes of everyone affected or decisions based on it will not be considered valid. The primary tool for project evaluation is the project audit, which is usually conducted at major milestones throughout the life of the project.

Purposes of Project Evaluation

Sports teams that practice without reviewing performance may get really good at playing very badly. That is why they review game films—to see where they need to improve.

As W. Edwards Deming has pointed out, there are two kinds of organizations—those that are getting better and those that are dying. An organization that stands still is dying. It just doesn't know it yet.

The reason? Your competitors are not sitting by idly. They are doing new things, some of which might be better than yours. If you aren't improving, you will be passed by, and soon you won't have a market.

The same is true of every part of an organization. You can't suboptimize, improving just manufacturing, for example. You have to improve every aspect of the business, and that includes how you run projects.

In fact, good project management can give you a real competitive advantage, especially in product development. If you are sloppy in managing your projects, you don't have good control of development costs. That means that you have to sell a lot of product or else charge large margins to cover your development costs so that the project is worth doing in

In order to learn, people require feedback. Furthermore, people tend to learn more from mistakes than from successes, painful though that may be to admit.

the first place. If you can't sell a lot of widgets, then you have to charge the large margin.

If your competitors, on the other hand, have good cost control, they can charge smaller margins and still be sure that they recover their investment and make money. They have a competitive advantage over you because of their better control of project work.

In order to learn, people, like the team reviewing game films, require feedback. The last phase of a project should be a final audit so that the management of future projects can be improved. However, such an audit should not be conducted only at the end of the project. Audits should be done at major milestones in the project so that learning can take place as the job progresses. Another reason to do periodic audits is that, if a project is getting into serious trouble, the audit should reveal the difficulty so that a decision can be made whether to continue or to terminate the work.

Periodic audits should enable you to:

- Improve project performance together with the management of the project.
- Ensure that quality of project work does not take a back seat to schedule and cost concerns.
- Reveal developing problems early so that action can be taken to deal with them.
- Identify areas where other projects (current or future) should be managed differently.
- Keep client(s) informed of project status. This can also help ensure that the completed project will meet the needs of the client.
- Reaffirm the organization's commitment to the project for the benefit of project team members.

Audits conducted like witch hunts will produce witches.

Conducting the Project Audit

Ideally, a project audit should be conducted by an independent examiner, who can remain objective in the assessment of information. However, the audit must be conducted in a spirit of learning, rather than in a climate of blame and punishment. If people are afraid that they will be "strung up" for problems, then they will hide those problems if at all possible. Such a benign atmosphere, however, is hard to achieve. In many organizations the climate has been punitive for so long that people are reluctant to reveal any less-than-perfect aspects of project performance. Dr. Chris Argyris, in his book *Overcoming Organizational Defenses,* has described the processes by which organizations continue ineffective practices. All of them are intended to help individuals "save face" or avoid embarrassment. In the end, they also prevent organizational learning.

Simply put, an auditor with a blame-and-punishment mentality is certain to create more problems than solutions.

The Audit Report

Audits come in different styles—comprehensive, partial, and informal and cursory. A formal, comprehensive audit should be followed by a report that, at a minimum, contains:

1. *Current project status.* This is best shown by performing an earned value analysis (see Chapter 8). However, when earned value analysis is not used, status should still be reported as accurately as possible.

2. *Future status.* This is a forecast of what is expected to happen in the project. Are significant deviations expected in schedule, cost, performance, or scope? If so, the nature of such changes should be specified.

3. *Status of critical tasks.* The status of critical tasks, particularly those on the critical path, should be reported. Tasks that have high levels of technical risk should be given special attention, as should those being performed by outside vendors or subcontractors, over which the project manager may have limited control.

4. *Risk assessment.* Have any risks been identified that highlight potential for monetary loss, project failure, or other liabilities?

5. *Information relevant to other projects.* What has been learned from this audit that can or should be applied to other projects, whether in progress or about to start?

6. *Limitations of the audit.* What factors might limit the validity of the audit? Are any assumptions suspect? Are any data missing or suspected of contamination? Was anyone uncooperative in providing information for the audit?

In general, the simpler and more straightforward a project audit report, the better. The information should be organized so that planned versus actual results can be easily compared, and significant deviations should be highlighted and explained.

Key Points to Remember

- The meaning of control that is important to project managers is the one that implies the use of information— comparing progress to plan so that corrective action can be taken to correct for deviations from plan.
- The only way a project will really be under control is if every team member is in control of his or her own work.
- The effort used to control a project should be worthwhile. You don't want to spend $100 to purchase a $3 battery, for example.
- If you do not react in response to a deviation, you have a monitoring system, not a control system.
- Project working times must be recorded daily. If people wait a week to capture what they have done, they rely on memory and end up writing down only their estimates of what they actually did. Such data are no good for future estimating.
- Project evaluation can help you determine whether a project should continue or be canceled. Audits also should help the team learn in order to improve performance.

CHAPTER 8

PROJECT CONTROL USING EARNED VALUE ANALYSIS

The goal of exercising control is to achieve project objectives; there are cost, time, performance, and scope targets that are always important. As we have noted, we exercise control to bring performance back on target by comparing performance to plan and taking corrective actions when deviations or variances occur.

One of the hardest things to do in managing projects is to actually measure progress. When you are following a road map, you monitor the road signs to check whether you are in fact following your planned route. Similarly, in well-defined jobs, such as some construction projects, it is generally fairly easy to tell where you are. You can measure the height of a brick wall or see if all the conduit is installed, and so on. That is, you can tell where you are when a part of the work is actually finished. When work is poorly defined and is only partially complete, however, you have to estimate where you are. This is especially true of knowledge work—work done with the head, rather than the hands. If you are writing software code, designing something, or writing a book, it can be very hard to judge how far along you are and how much you have left to do.

Naturally, if you can't tell where you are, you can't exercise control. Note the word *estimate* in measuring progress. What, exactly, is an estimate?

It's a guess.

And so we are guessing about where we are. We'll know where we are when we get there. Until we actually arrive, we're guessing.

Does this not sound like something from *Alice in Wonderland?* Now, what was that definition of control again? Let's see—compare where you are . . .

How do you know where you are?

We're guessing.

. . . against where you are supposed to be . . .

How do you know where you're supposed to be?

Oh, that's much easier. The plan tells us.

But where did the plan come from?

It was an estimate, too.

Oh. So if one guess doesn't agree with the other guess, we're supposed to take corrective action to make the two of them agree, is that it?

That's what this guy Jim Lewis says in his book.

Must be a book on witchcraft and magic.

Well, since it is impossible to know for sure where we are, then perhaps we should just give up on the whole thing and keep running projects by the seat of the pants. Right?

Wrong.

The difficulty of measuring progress does not justify the conclusion that progress shouldn't be measured. You cannot have control unless you measure progress.

The fact that planning and monitoring progress may not always be accurate does not justify the conclusion that they shouldn't be done. Remember, if you have no plan, you have no control, and if you don't try to monitor and follow the plan, you definitely don't have control. And if you have no control, there is no semblance of managing. You're just flailing around.

What is important to note, however, is that some projects are capable of tighter control than others. Work that can be accurately measured can be controlled to tight tolerances. Work that is more nebulous (such as knowledge work) has to allow larger tolerances. Management must recognize this reality and accept it. Otherwise, people will go crazy trying to achieve 3 percent tolerances. It's like trying to push a noodle in a straight line or nail jelly to a wall.

MEASURING PROJECT PERFORMANCE/ QUALITY

If you think measuring progress is hard, try measuring quality. Were the bolts holding the steel beams together put in properly? Are all the welds sound? How do you tell?

Quality is the hardest variable to track, and the one that often suffers as a consequence. In addition, so much attention tends to be focused on cost and schedule performance that work quality is often sacrificed. This can be a disaster, in some cases resulting in customer lawsuits for damages resulting from poor-quality products.

Project managers must pay special attention to the quality variable, in spite of the difficulty of tracking it.

EARNED VALUE ANALYSIS

It is one thing to meet a project deadline at any cost. It is another to do it for a reasonable cost. Project cost control is concerned with ensuring that projects stay within their budgets, while getting the work done on time and with the correct degree of quality. One system for measuring these factors is called *earned value analysis* (also known as *variance analysis)*, which was developed in the 1960s to allow the government to decide if a contractor should receive a progress payment for work done. The method is finally coming into its own outside of government projects, and it is considered the correct way to monitor and control almost any project. Variance analysis allows the project manager to determine "trouble spots" in the project and to take corrective action.

Terms Used in Earned Value Analysis

- *Cost Variance:* Measures the gap between the budgeted cost and the actual cost of performed work.
- *Schedule Variance:* Compares planned versus actual work completed.

- *Budgeted Cost of Work Scheduled (BCWS):* The budgeted cost of work scheduled to be done in a given time period, or the level of effort supposed to be expended during that period.
- *Budgeted Cost of Work Performed (BCWP):* The budgeted cost of work actually performed in a given period, or the budgeted level of effort actually expended. BCWP, also called earned value, is a measure of the dollar value of the work actually accomplished in the period being monitored.
- *Actual Cost of Work Performed (ACWP):* The amount of money (or effort) actually spent in completing work in a given period.

Variance thresholds can be established to define the level at which reports must be sent to various levels of management within an organization.

By combining cost and schedule variances, an integrated cost/schedule reporting system can be developed. Two formulas are of use in performing earned value analysis using these concepts:

$$Cost\ variance = BCWP - ACWP$$
$$Schedule\ variance = BCWP - BCWS$$

Earned Value Analysis Using Spending Curves

Variances are often plotted using spending curves. Figure 8-1 shows a BCWS curve for a project. This graph shows the cumulative spending planned for a project and is sometimes called a baseline plan.

In case you do not have available software to provide the necessary data, we show in Figure 8-2 how to generate the data for the curve. Consider a simple bar-chart schedule. Only three tasks are involved. Task 1 involves forty labor-hours per week at an average loaded labor rate of $20 per hour, so that task spends $800/week. Task 2 involves one hundred hours per week of labor at $30 per hour, for a cost

Figure 8-1.   Cumulative spending curve.

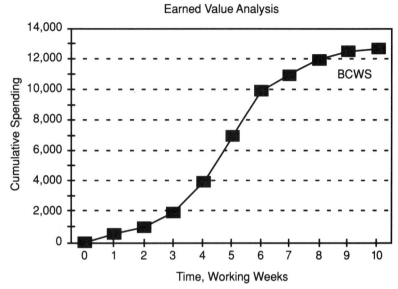

Figure 8-2.   Bar chart schedule illustrating cumulative spending.

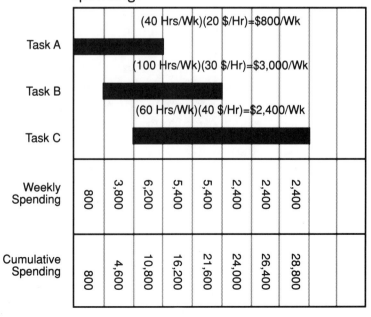

of $3,000 per week. Finally, task 3 costs $2,400 per week, based on sixty hours per week of labor at $40 per hour.

At the bottom of the chart we see that during the first week $800 is spent for project labor; in the second week, both tasks 1 and 2 are running, so the labor expenditure is $3,800. In the third week, all three tasks are running, so labor expenditure is the sum of the three, or $6,200. These are the weekly expenditures.

The cumulative expenditures are calculated by adding the cost for each subsequent week to the previous cumulative total. These cumulative amounts are plotted in Figure 8-3. This is the spending curve for the project and is called a BCWS curve. Since it is derived directly from the schedule, it represents *planned performance* and therefore is called a *baseline plan*. Because control is exercised by comparing actual progress to planned progress, this curve can be used as the basis for such comparisons.

Examples of Progress Tracking Using Spending Curves

Consider the curves shown in Figure 8-4. On a given date, the project is supposed to have cost $50,000 (50K) in labor (BCWS). The actual cost of the work performed (ACWP) is 60K. (These figures are usually obtained from Accounting and are derived from all of the time cards that have reported labor applied to the project.) Finally, the budgeted cost of work performed (BCWP) is 40K. Under these conditions, the project would be behind schedule and overspent.

Figure 8-5 illustrates another scenario. In this case, the BCWP and the ACWP curves both fall at the same point, that is, at 60K. This means that the project is ahead of schedule but spending correctly for the amount of work done.

The next set of curves illustrates another possibility. In Figure 8-6 the BCWP and the ACWP curves are both at 40K. This means the project is behind schedule and under budget. However, because the project spending is 40K and

Figure 8-3. Cumulative spending for sample bar chart.

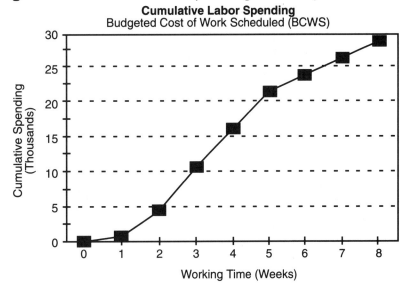

Figure 8-4. Earned value analysis—behind schedule, overspent.

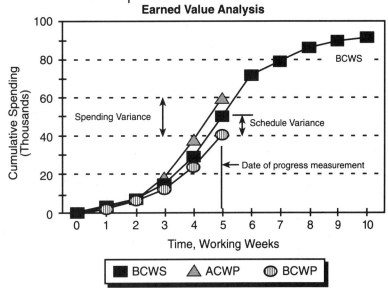

Figure 8-5. Earned value analysis—ahead of schedule, spending on target.

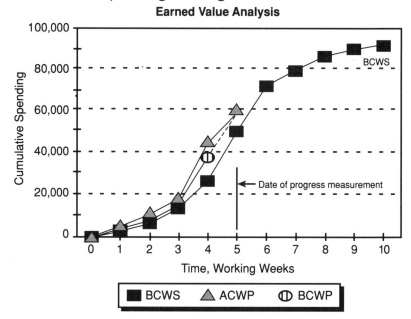

Figure 8-6. Earned value analysis—behind schedule, spending on target.

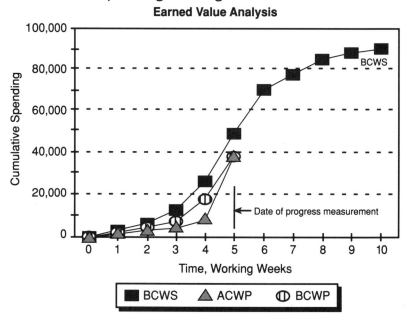

work value is 40K, spending is correct for what is being accomplished. There is a schedule variance but not a spending variance.

In our last example, shown in Figure 8-7, the graph looks like that in Figure 8-4, except that the ACWP and the BCWP curves have been reversed. Now the project is ahead of schedule and underspent.

Earned Value Analysis Using Hours Only

In some organizations, project managers are held accountable not for costs but only for the hours actually worked on the project and for the work actually accomplished. In this case, earned value analysis can be conducted by stripping the dollars off the figures. This results in the following changes:

> BCWS becomes Total Planned (or Scheduled) Hours
> BCWP becomes Earned Hours (Scheduled hours × % work accomplished)
> ACWP becomes Actual Hours Worked *(Actual Labor hours)*

Figure 8-7.   Earned value analysis—ahead of schedule, underspent.

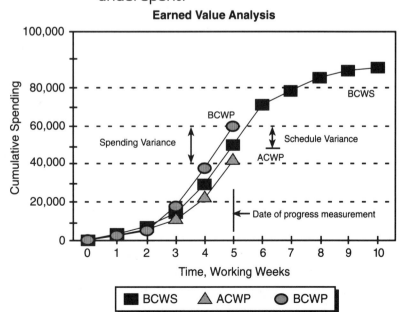

Using hours only, the formulas become:

$$Schedule\ Variance = BCWP - BCWS$$
$$= Earned\ Hours - Planned\ Hours$$
$$Labor\ Variance = BCWP - ACWP$$
$$= Earned\ Hours - Actual\ Hours\ Worked$$

Tracking hours only does lead to some loss of sensitivity. ACWP is actually the composite of a labor rate variance times a labor hours variance. When only labor hours are tracked, you have no warning that labor rates might cause a project budget problem. Nevertheless, this method does simplify the analysis and presumably tracks the project manager only on what she can control.

RESPONDING TO VARIANCES

It is not enough simply to detect a variance. The next step is to understand what it means and what caused it. Then you have to decide what to do to correct for the deviation. Following are some general guidelines.

• When ACWP and BCWP are almost equal and larger than BCWS (see Figure 8-5), it usually means that extra resources have been applied to the project, but at the labor rates originally anticipated. This can happen in several ways. Perhaps you planned for weather delays, but the weather has been good and you have gotten more work done during the analysis period than intended but at the correct cost. Thus, you are ahead of schedule but spending correctly.

• When ACWP and BCWP are nearly equal and below BCWS (see Figure 8-6), it usually means the opposite of the previous situation; that is, you have not had enough resources applied. Perhaps resources were stolen from you, perhaps it has rained more than you expected, or perhaps everyone has decided to take a vacation at once. The problem with being in this position is that it usually results in an overspend when you try to catch up.

• When ACWP is below BCWS and BCWP is above BCWS (see Figure 8-7), you are ahead of schedule and underspent. This generally happens because the original estimate was too conservative (probably padded for safety). Another possibility is that you had a lucky break. You thought the work would be harder than it was, so you got ahead. Sometimes it happens because people worked much more efficiently than you expected. The problem with this variance is that it ties up resources that could have been used on other projects. The economists call this an opportunity cost.

There is also a good chance that if you consistently pad estimates and bid against other companies on projects, you will probably lose some bids, especially if your competitor is using average values for time estimates while you are padding yours.

Measuring Progress Using Percent Complete

The most common way to measure progress is simply to estimate *percent complete*. This is the BCWP measure, but BCWP is expressed as a dollar value, whereas percent complete does not make that conversion.

When percent complete measures are plotted over time, they often produce a curve like the one shown in Figure 8-8. The curve rises more or less linearly up to about 80 or 90 percent, then turns horizontal (meaning that no further progress is being made). The curve stays horizontal for a while, until all of a sudden the work is completed.

The reason for this common profile is that problems are often encountered near the end of the task, requiring a lot of effort to solve them. While that is being done, no progress is being made toward completing the project.

Another part of the problem is in knowing where you are to begin with. We have already said that you are generally estimating progress. Consider a task that has a ten-week duration. If you ask the person doing that task where he is

Figure 8-8.   Percent complete curve.

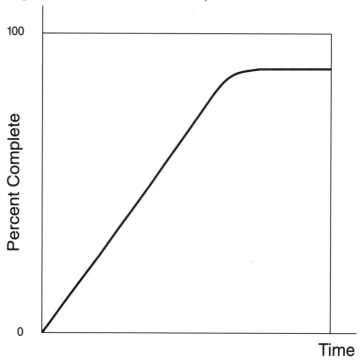

at the end of the first week, he is likely to tell you, "I'm 10 percent along." At the end of week 2, he'll probably say, "About 20 percent finished." And so on. What he is doing is making a reverse inference. It goes like this. "It is the end of the first week on a ten-week task, so I must be 10 percent complete." The truth is, he really doesn't know where he is. Naturally, under such conditions, control will be very loose. Still, it is the only way progress can be measured in many cases.

What Are Acceptable Variances?

The only answer that can be given to this question is, "It all depends." If you are doing a well-defined construction job, the variances can be in the range of ±3 to 5 percent. If it is research and development, it goes up generally to around ±10 to 15 percent. If the project involves pure research, the sky is the limit. Imagine, for example, that you work for a pharmaceutical company, and your boss says, "Tell me how long it will take and how much it will cost for you to discover and develop a cure for AIDS."

For every organization, you will have to develop a sense of acceptable tolerances through experience. Then you start trying to reduce them. All progress is an attempt to reduce variation in what we do. We will never reduce variation to zero without eliminating the process altogether, but zero has to be the target.

EXERCISE

Figure 8-9 shows earned value figures for a project. Answer the questions by analyzing the data. Answers are provided in the Appendix.

Questions:

- Is the task ahead or behind schedule? By how much?
- Is the task overspent or underspent? By how much?
- When the task is completed, will it be overspent or underspent?

Figure 8-9. Earned value report.

	Cumulative-to-date			Variance		At Completion		
WBS#	BCWS	BCWP	ACWP	Sched.	Cost	Budget	L. Est.	Var'nce
301	800	640	880	−160	−240	2,400	2,816	−416

Key Points to Remember

- Control is exercised by analyzing variances from the plan.
- Well-defined projects can achieve tighter control over variations than can poorly defined ones.
- There is a tendency to sacrifice quality when deadlines are difficult to meet.
- It is not enough to recognize a variance. Its cause must be determined so that corrective action can be taken.
- Acceptable variances can be determined only through experience. Every system has its own level of capability. Your team may have the ability to hold better tolerances on its work than another team.

CHAPTER 9

MANAGING THE PROJECT TEAM

In previous chapters I have concentrated primarily on the tools of project management—how to plan, schedule, and control the work. Unfortunately, far too many project managers see these tools as all they need to manage successfully. They assemble a team, give the members their instructions, and sit back and watch the project self-destruct. Then they question whether there might have been some flaw in the tools.

In all likelihood, the problem was with how people were managed. Even in those cases where a problem with the tools might have existed, it is often the failure of people to apply them properly that causes the problem, bringing us again back to people.

Having the tools and techniques of project management is a necessary but not a sufficient condition for project success. As I have stated, if you can't handle people, you will have difficulty managing projects, especially when the people don't "belong" to you.

Related to this is the need to turn a project group into a team. Far too little attention is paid to team building in project management. This chapter offers some suggestions on how to go about it.

Teams don't just happen— they must be built!

TEAM BUILDING BEGINS ON DAY ONE

Building an effective team begins on the first day of the team's existence. Failure to begin the team-building process may result in something more like a group than a team. In a group, members may be involved in, but not committed to, the activities of the majority.

The problem of commitment is a major one for both organizations and project teams. It is especially significant in matrix organizations, in which members of the project team are actually members of functional groups and have their own bosses but report to the project manager on a "dotted-line" basis.

Later in this chapter, I present rules to help project managers develop commitment among team members. For now, let us turn to ways to get a team organized so that it gets off to the right start. (For an in-depth treatment of this topic, see my book *How to Build and Manage a Winning Project Team*.)

PROMOTING TEAMWORK THROUGH PLANNING

A primary rule of planning is that those individuals who must implement the plan should participate in preparing it. Yet leaders often plan projects by themselves, then wonder why their team members seem to have no commitment to the plans.

All planning requires some estimating—for example, how long a task will take, given certain resources. In my seminars, I ask participants, "Do you often find that your boss thinks you can do your work much faster than you actually can?" They laugh and agree. It seems to be some kind of psychological law that bosses are optimistic about how long it will take their people to get a job done.

When a manager gives a person an inadequate amount of time to complete an assignment, the individual naturally feels discouraged, and her commitment is likely to suffer. She might say, "I'll give it my best shot," but her heart won't really be in it.

GETTING ORGANIZED

There are four essential steps in getting a new project team organized:

1. Decide what must be done, using work breakdown structure, problem definitions, and other planning tools.
2. Determine the staffing required to accomplish the tasks identified in step 1.
3. Recruit members for the project team.
4. Complete your project plan through the participation of team members.

Some of the criteria by which team members should be selected include:

- The candidate should possess the necessary skills to perform the required work at the speed needed to meet deadlines.
- The candidate should have his needs met through participation in the project (see the March and Simon rules later in this chapter).
- The applicant should have the temperament to fit in with other team members who have already been recruited, as well as with the project manager and other key players.
- The person should not object to overtime requirements, tight timetables, or other project work requirements.

TEAM ISSUES

All teams must grapple with four essential issues: clarifying mission, goals, and objectives; defining roles and responsibilities; working out procedures; and managing interpersonal relationships.

Clarifying the Team's Mission, Goals, and Objectives

Excellent organizations, as I have noted, stick to what they are good at and do not get off on tangents, trying to do something they know nothing about. (Imagine, as an example, a hockey team deciding to play basketball.)

Numerous case studies and articles have been written about organizations that got off on tangents, at great cost, because they forgot their mission. The same can happen to project teams. If members are not clear on the team's mission, they will take the team where they think it is supposed to go, which may not be the direction intended by the organization. I have discussed the procedure for developing a mission statement in Chapter 3; working with your team to develop a mission statement is a good team-building activity in itself.

Conflicts Between Individual Goals and the Team's Mission

Team members are most committed to a team when their individual needs are being met. Sometimes members have what are called hidden agendas—personal objectives that they do not want anyone to know about, because they are afraid other members will try to block them if their objectives are known. Since a manager should try to help individual members achieve their personal goals while also achieving team goals, the team leader needs to bring hidden agendas into the open so that the individual can be assisted in achieving his goal. Of course, a person may occasionally have a goal that runs so counter to the team's goals that no reconciliation is possible. In that case, if the team leader can discover what the person's goal is, the individual should ideally be moved to another team in which his goal can be reached.

Understanding Roles and Responsibilities

Once the team's goals and mission have been established, people's roles must be clearly defined. What is expected of each individual, and by when? One common problem is that team leaders think they communicate information on goals and roles clearly to team members, yet team members remain fuzzy on these critical areas.

The problem is that we fail to solicit feedback from team members to be really sure that they understand their roles and responsibilities and that team members themselves are sometimes reluctant to admit that they don't understand. This reluctance appears to be a result of our tendency in school to put people down for asking "stupid" questions. So, as adults, rather than admit that they don't understand, people interpret what they have been told and try to do the job the best they can.

Project leaders must establish a climate of open communication with the team, a climate in which no one feels too intimidated to speak up. The best way to do this is to comment on the problem: "I know some of you may feel reluctant to speak up and say you don't understand, but we can't operate that way. Please feel free to be candid. If you don't understand, say so. If you don't agree with something, say so. That is the only way we can succeed. We will be lucky to have time to do the job once, much less find time to do it over because one of you failed to understand what was expected."

I have also found that people respond very positively when I am willing to admit that I don't understand something myself or am apprehensive or concerned about a project issue. If you project an air of infallibility, no one else is likely to admit a weakness. But then, who wants to deal with a demigod? A little human frailty goes a long way toward breaking down barriers. I know this contradicts what some managers have been taught. The macho notion of infallibility has been with us for a long time, and I believe it is the cause of many of our organizational problems. It is time to abandon it for reality.

Working Out Procedures

Dealing with how to do the project work is the third issue with which teams must grapple. The work must be done as efficiently and effectively as possible. Trying constantly to improve work processes is a very important issue today. Commonly called reengineering, this effort requires the analysis and improvement of work processes to make the organization more competitive.

The difficulty that most teams have with process is that they get so focused on doing the work that they forget to examine how it is done. Periodically a team should stop working long enough to examine its processes and see if there are better approaches that could be used. Otherwise, it may get very good at doing the work badly.

Managing Interpersonal Relationships

Friction exists in almost any interaction between human beings. There may be misunderstandings, conflicts, personality clashes, or petty jealousies. Project managers must be prepared to deal with all of these. In fact, if you dislike having to deal with the behavioral problems that arise on project teams, you should ask yourself whether you really want to manage projects at all. Like it or not, the behavioral problems come with the job, and failure to deal with them may sink a project.

Many personality clashes are the result of a lack of good interpersonal skills. People have never been taught how to sit down and work out differences with others, so when the inevitable conflict happens, it just blows up. The best way to minimize the impact of such problems is to provide training for all team members (including yourself) in interpersonal skills. This area has been sorely neglected in many organizations because there seems to be no bottom-line impact. It is hard to prove that there will be a $10 return on a $1 training investment.

Because of their inability to quantify the benefits, companies don't do the training. Yet if they have capital resources that don't work well, they will spend whatever is necessary to correct the problem. Interestingly, a company's human resources are the only ones that are renewable almost indefi-

The most popular terms for the stages of team development are: forming storming norming performing

nitely, but companies fail to take steps to keep them functioning effectively. As a project manager, you owe it to yourself to manage this aspect of the job.

STAGES IN A TEAM'S DEVELOPMENT

There are a number of models that describe the stages through which teams or groups pass on the way to maturity. One of the more popular ones has self-explanatory titles for the stages: forming, storming, norming, and performing.

In the *forming* stage, people are concerned with how they will fit in, who calls the shots and makes decisions, and so on. During this stage they look to the leader (or someone else) to give them some structure—that is, to give them a sense of direction and to help them get started. Failure of the leader to do this may result in losing the team to some member who exercises what we call informal leadership.

In the *storming* stage, people begin to question their goals. Are they on the right track? Is the leader really leading them? They sometimes play shoot-the-leader during this stage. The storming stage is frustrating for most people.

In the *norming* stage team members begin to resolve their conflicts and to settle down to work. They have developed norms (unwritten rules) about how they will work together, and they feel more comfortable with each other. Each individual has found his place in the team and knows what to expect of the others.

When the team members reach the *performing* stage, the leader's job is easier. Team members generally work well together now, enjoy doing so, and tend to produce high-quality results. They can really be called a team at this point.

Leading a Team Through the Four Stages

A newly formed team needs considerable structure, or it will not be able to get started. As I noted in the previous section, a leader who fails to provide such structure may be rejected

A *directive* style of leadership is called for when a team is in the forming stage.

by the group, which will look for leadership from someone else. A *directive* style of leadership is called for in the forming stage.

During the forming stage, members also want to get to know each other and want to understand the role each member will play in the team. The leader must therefore help team members get to know each other and to understand clearly the team's goals, roles, and responsibilities. One error that may be made by very task-oriented leaders is to tell the team to "get to work," without helping members get to know each other; such leaders tend to view purely "social" activities as a waste of time. It should be obvious, however, that it is hard to see yourself as a team when you don't know some of the "players."

Getting the team started with a kick-off party or dinner is one way to let members get to know one another in a purely social way, with no pressure to perform actual task work. If this is not feasible, you must find some mechanism for letting people get to know one another.

As the group continues to develop, it enters the storming stage. Here, people are beginning to have some anxiety. They start to question the group's goal and wonder whether they are doing what they're supposed to be doing. The leader must use *influence* or persuasion to assure them that they are indeed on track. Members need a lot of psychological support, as well. They must be assured by the leader that they are valued and that they are vital to the success of the team. In other words, some stroking is needed in this stage.

A *selling* or *influence* style of leadership is appropriate at the storming stage.

There is a tendency to try to skip this second stage, as we feel uncomfortable with the conflict that occurs. To sweep such conflict under the rug and pretend that it doesn't exist is a mistake. The conflict must be managed so that it does not become destructive, but it must not be avoided. If it is, the group will keep coming back to this stage to try to resolve the conflict, and this will inhibit its progress. Better to pay now and get it over with.

In the norming stage, the leader should adopt a *participative* style of leadership.

As the team enters the norming stage, it becomes more close knit. Members begin to see themselves as a team and take some sense of personal identity from membership in the group. They are now involved in the work, are becoming supportive of each other, and, because of their cooperation, can be said to be more of a team than a group at this point. The leader needs to adopt a *participative* style with team members in this stage and to share decision making more than in the first two stages.

By the time a group reaches stage four, performing, it is a real team. The leader can generally sit back and concentrate on doing what-if analysis of team progress, planning for future work, and so on. This is a *delegative* style of leadership, and it is very appropriate. The team is achieving results, and members are usually taking pride in their accomplishments. In this stage, there should be signs of camaraderie, joking around, and real enjoyment in working together.

It is important to remember that no team stays in a single stage forever. If a team encounters obstacles, it may drop back to stage three. If this happens, the leader can no longer be delegative but must back up to the stage-three management style, which is participative.

Delegative leadership is the proper style in the performing stage of a team's development. Note that *delegative* does not mean abdication!

The other thing that happens is that membership in project teams often changes. When new members come on board, you should consider that for a short time the team will fall back to stage one, and you have to take them back through the stages until they reach maturity again. It is especially important that you help everyone get to know the new member and understand what her role will be in the team. This does take some time, but it is essential if you want the team to progress properly.

DEVELOPING COMMITMENT TO A TEAM

At the beginning of this chapter, I pointed out that helping team members develop commitment to the project team is a major problem for project managers. Team members are often assigned to a project simply because they are the best person, not because they are the best person for the job. When this happens, commitment to the team may be non-existent.

James March and Herbert Simon, in their book *Organizations,* presented five rules for developing commitment to a team or organization. They are:

1. Have team members interact frequently so that they gain a sense of being a team.
2. Be sure that individual needs are being met through participation in the team.
3. Let team members all know why the project is important. People don't like working on a "loser."
4. Make sure all members share the goals of the team. One bad apple can spoil the barrel.
5. Keep competition within the team to a minimum. Competition and cooperation are opposites. Let the team compete with people outside the team, not within it.

Note that the first rule is hard to follow if the team is scattered geographically. In that case, the members should "meet" frequently through teleconferencing. It is almost impossible to think of yourself as part of a team if you never get together in some manner.

RULES FOR DEVELOPING COMMITMENT TO A PROJECT TEAM

- Have team members interact frequently, so they gain a sense of being a team.
- Be sure that individual needs are being met through participation in the team.
- Let them all know why the project is important. People don't like working on a "loser."
- Make sure all members share the goals of the team. One bad "apple" can spoil the barrel.
- Keep competition within the team to a minimum. Competition and cooperation are opposites. Let them compete with people outside the team, not within it.

A FINAL SUGGESTION

If you want some good models of how to work with teams, take a look at the best coaches and see how they do it. Be careful, though, not to model the super-macho coach's behavior. That style might work with a sports team, where people are there because they want to be there, but it is unlikely to work well with a project team where the members are there because they have to be. I also suggest that you watch the movie *Stand and Deliver* (available on video) and see how Jaime Escalante deals with his kids. This movie presents the true story of how teacher Jaime Escalante achieved exceptional results with a class of math students who would ordinarily be called *disadvantaged*. Then, the next time you are tempted to complain that you have a lot of responsibility and no authority, ask yourself how a teacher (who has even less authority than you do) can get a bunch of kids to work so hard. How did he get them to go to summer school or to take math two periods a day? Then you will begin to realize what true leadership is all about.

Key Points to Remember

- Teams don't just happen—they must be built!
- Having the entire team participate in planning is one way to start the team-building process.
- Deal with goals, roles and responsibilities, procedures, and relationships in that order.
- So-called personality conflicts are often nothing but the result of poor interpersonal skills. For teams to function well, all members should receive training in this area.
- The style of leadership appropriate for a team depends on the team's stage of development. In the forming stage, it is directive. In storming, it requires influence. At the norming stage, leadership is participative. In the performing stage, it is delegative.

CHAPTER 10

HOW TO MAKE PROJECT MANAGEMENT WORK IN YOUR COMPANY

It is one thing to know how to manage projects effectively. It is another to get people actually to manage them that way. Running by the seat of the pants seems a lot easier than doing all that planning, scheduling, and monitoring. Even when people invest three or four days in project management seminars, you find that they soon forget what they have been taught and go back to the old ways.

I have struggled with this problem for over fifteen years, and I finally have some answers. Here are suggestions on how to make the principles of project management work in your company.

• Dr. Edwards Deming learned more than fifty years ago that if you don't get top management involved in a program, the program will be short-lived. That doesn't mean just having top management pay lip service to it. As Tom Peters suggested in his book *Thriving on Chaos,* if an executive wants something to happen in the company she has to change her calendar! Spend time talking about project management. Sit in on project planning or review meetings. Start asking to see people's project notebooks. Ask questions about how projects are doing. In other words, show an interest in the subject.

• Build into performance appraisals items that evaluate a project manager's use of the tools of effective project management. Reward people for practicing the methods. If necessary, sanction them when they do not. But be careful.

109

Be sure upper management is not keeping managers from practicing good methodology.

- It helps to have the entire team trained in the basics. After all, when you tell members of your team you want them to do a WBS for their part of the project and they have never even heard the term before, they can't very well deliver. I have found that project managers generally need a minimum of three or four days' training in project management, and team members need about two days' training to learn just the tools.

- Senior management should have a one-day overview of the principles of project management so that it knows what is realistic to expect. One of the ten most common causes of project failures is unrealistic expectations on the part of senior managers.

- After the training is complete, pick a project that already has a pretty high probability of success. Don't pick your hardest job; it has too high a likelihood of failure—and have your trainer/consultant walk the team through the steps. This is the hand-holding phase, which I have found to be essential (as have a number of major companies with which I have worked). It really helps to have someone help the team practice what it has learned. All new procedures feel awkward when you first try them, and an outside expert makes things go smoother. In addition, an outsider can be more objective than members of the team.

- Plan small wins for people. Forget the Pareto principle. It's wrong, even from an economic point of view. According to Pareto, you should begin with your most important problems, solve them, and then move on to the simpler ones. Sounds like good economic sense, but it isn't. It ignores the fact that the biggest problem is also likely to be the hardest to tackle, so people are more likely to fail, become demoralized, and give up. No sports team ranked tenth would want to play the top-ranked team for its first game. It would rather play the ninth-ranked team, maybe, or even the eleventh. Don't set the team up to be slaughtered!

- Practice a lot of MBWA (management by walking around) as the project progresses, but do it to be helpful, not in the blame-and-punishment mode. Give people strokes for letting you know about problems early, rather than after they have turned into disasters. Don't be too quick to help, though. Give people time to solve the problems themselves. Just ask them to keep you informed, and tell them to let you know if they need help. Be a resource, not a policeman.

• Do audits to learn, and try to improve whenever possible.

• If you find you have a problem individual on your team, deal with that person as soon as possible. If you don't know how to handle the problem, talk to someone who has the experience and who can help you. Don't ignore the problem, as it can wreck your entire team.

• Be very pro-active, not reactive. Take the lead. Break roadblocks for your team members. Go to bat for them.

• Have team members make presentations to senior management on their part of the job. Give them credit for their contributions. Build ownership.

• If you are running a project to which people are temporarily assigned while still reporting to their own bosses (matrix organization), keep their managers informed about what they are doing. Try to build good relations with those managers. You may need their support to get the job done.

• You may find that you have to co-locate the people doing activities on the project's critical path so that you don't have them constantly pulled off to do other jobs. This method is being used more and more by major corporations for highly critical projects.

• It may be useful to consider setting up a project support person or office to do all scheduling for your project managers. Rather than have everyone trying to master the scheduling software, it might be better to train one or two people to competence level and to train users only enough to know the capability of the software. Under this scenario, project managers give raw data to the support group, who enter it into the computer and give back a proposed schedule, which is then massaged until it works. Subsequently the support group does all updates, what-if analyses, and so on for the project manager.

• It is also possible to appoint a project administrator to either do the project support or delegate it and to sit in on project review meetings and hold the team's hands to walk members through planning, audits, and so forth. Naturally, you need to be running quite a few projects (at least ten to twenty) to justify creating this position. Such a position can be helpful when you have project managers who have little experience with managing or who perhaps have poor skills in dealing with people, or both.

• Benchmark other companies to find out what they do with project management. Note that the fact that others don't practice good methodology does not give you grounds for abandoning it yourself. I know of one major corporation that does not track actual work put into a project; yet the company is extremely successful. However, I believe that because the company doesn't track work, it will lead to problems eventually.

• Have individuals take responsibility for championing various parts of the project management process. One person, for example, the earned-value champion, might go around the company trying to get everyone to use the method. Another might take responsibility for dealing with WBS notation, and so on.

• Join the Project Management Institute, attend chapter meetings, and learn more about the practice from other professionals.

• Try to read current management books, and glean everything you can from them that will help you do your job better. Managing projects is a demanding job, and you need all the help you can get.

• Look at managing projects as a challenge or even as a game. If it doesn't strike you that way, it probably won't be very exciting. Experiment with new approaches. Find out what works and keep it. Throw out what does not.

• Finally—good luck!

APPENDIX: ANSWERS TO CHAPTER EXERCISES

CHAPTER 2

1. **c**; 2. **a**; 3. **d**; 4. **d**; 5. **a**; 6. **b**

CHAPTER 4

Figure A-1. WBS for camping trip.

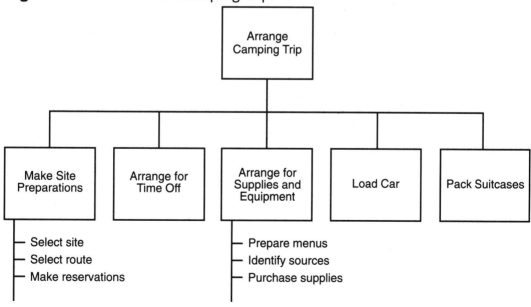

CHAPTER 5

Figure A-2.   Arrow diagram for house cleaning.

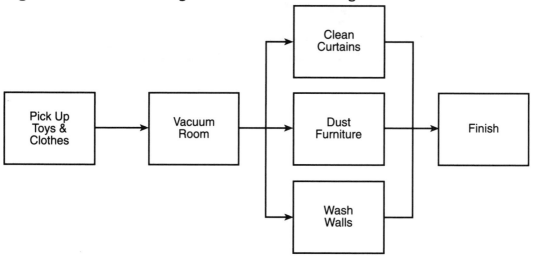

CHAPTER 6

Figure A-3.   Network solution.

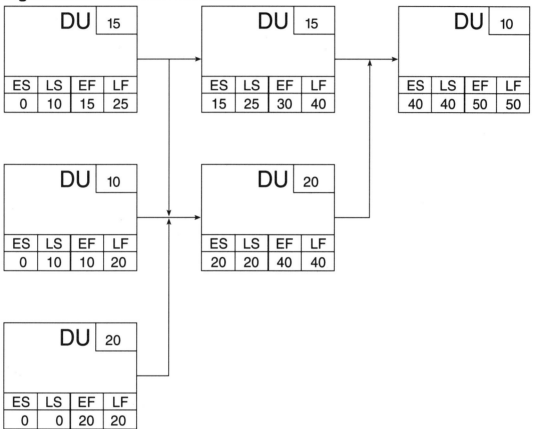

CHAPTER 8

1. Behind schedule, by $160 worth of work.
2. Overspent by $240.
3. Overspent by $416.

REFERENCES

Akao, Yoji, editor. *Quality Function Deployment: Integrating Customer Requirements into Product Design*. Cambridge, Mass.: Productivity Press, 1990.

Argyris, Chris. *Overcoming Organizational Defenses: Facilitating Organizational Learning*. Boston: Allyn and Bacon, 1990.

Hersey, Paul, and Kenneth Blanchard. *Management of Organizational Behavior: Utilizing Human Resources*, Fourth edition. Englewood Cliffs, N.J.: Prentice-Hall, 1981.

Lewis, James P. *How to Build and Manage a Winning Project Team*. New York: AMACOM, 1993.

Peters, Tom, and Bob Waterman. *In Search of Excellence: Lessons from America's Best Run Companies*. New York: Harper & Row, 1982.

Russo, J. Edward, and Paul J. H. Schoemaker. *Decision Traps: The Ten Barriers to Brilliant Decision-Making and How to Overcome Them*. New York: Fireside Books, 1989.

Schumacher, E. F. *Small Is Beautiful*. New York: Perennial Library, 1973.

Slevin, Dennis P. *The Whole Manager: How to Increase Your Professional and Personal Effectiveness*. New York: AMACOM, 1989.